BARRON'S BOOK NOTES

HENRIK IBSEN'S

A Doll's House & Hedda Gabler

BY

Sharon Linnea
Associate Editor, *Scholastic Voice*
Scholastic Inc.

SERIES COORDINATOR
Murray Bromberg
Principal, Wang High School of Queens
Holliswood, New York
Past President
High School Prin~~~~~~~~~~~~~~City

Avon ~~~~
326~~
Avon Lake, Ohio 44012

BARRON'S EDUCATIONAL SERIES, INC.

ACKNOWLEDGMENTS

Our thanks to Milton Katz and Julius Liebb for their advisory assistance on the *Book Notes* series.

© Copyright 1985 by Barron's Educational Series, Inc.

All inquiries should be addressed to:
Barron's Educational Series, Inc.
250 Wireless Boulevard
Hauppauge, New York 11788

Library of Congress Catalog Card No. 85-3999

International Standard Book No. 0-8120-3511-9

Library of Congress Cataloging in Publication Data
Linnea, Sharon.
    Henrik Ibsen's Hedda Gabler & A doll's house.

    (Barron's book notes)
    Bibliography: p. 116
    Summary: A guide to reading "Hedda Gabler"
and "A Doll's House" with a critical and
appreciative mind. Includes background on the
author's life and times, sample tests, term
paper suggestions, and a reading list.
    1. Ibsen, Henrik, 1828–1906. Hedda Gabler.
2. Ibsen, Henrik, 1828–1906. Dukkehjem.
[1. Ibsen, Henrik, 1828–1906. Hedda Gabler.
2. Ibsen, Henrik, 1828–1906. Doll's House.
3. Norwegian literature—History and criticism]
I. Title. II. Title: Henrik Ibsen's Hedda
Gabler and A doll's house. III. Series.
PT8868.L56 1985   839.8'226   85-3999
ISBN 0-8120-3511-9

PRINTED IN THE UNITED STATES OF AMERICA

123   550   98765432

CONTENTS

HOW TO USE THIS BOOK

You have to know how to approach literature in order to get the most out of it. This *Barron's Book Notes* volume follows a plan based on methods used by some of the best students to read a work of literature.

Begin with the guide's section on the author's life and times. As you read, try to form a clear picture of the author's personality, circumstances, and motives for writing the work. This background usually will make it easier for you to hear the author's tone of voice, and follow where the author is heading.

Then go over the rest of the introductory material—such sections as those on the plot, characters, setting, themes, and style of the work. Underline, or write down in your notebook, particular things to watch for, such as contrasts between characters and repeated literary devices. At this point, you may want to develop a system of symbols to use in marking your text as you read. (Of course, you should only mark up a book you own, not one that belongs to another person or a school.) Perhaps you will want to use a different letter for each character's name, a different number for each major theme of the book, a different color for each important symbol or literary device. Be prepared to mark up the pages of your book as you read. Put your marks in the margins so you can find them again easily.

Now comes the moment you've been waiting for—the time to start reading the work of literature. You may want to put aside your *Barron's Book Notes* volume until you've read the work all the way through. Or you may want to alternate, reading the *Book Notes* analysis of each section as soon as you have finished reading the corresponding part of the original. Before you move on, reread crucial passages you don't fully understand. (Don't take this guide's analysis for granted—make up your own mind as to what the work means.)

Once you've finished the whole work of literature, you may want to review it right away, so you can firm up your ideas about what it means. You may want to leaf through the book concentrating on passages you marked in reference to one character or one theme. This is also a good time to reread the *Book Notes* introductory material, which pulls together insights on specific topics.

When it comes time to prepare for a test or to write a paper, you'll already have formed ideas about the work. You'll be able to go back through it, refreshing your memory as to the author's exact words and perspective, so that you can support your opinions with evidence drawn straight from the work. Patterns will emerge, and ideas will fall into place; your essay question or term paper will almost write itself. Give yourself a dry run with one of the sample tests in the guide. These tests present both multiple-choice and essay questions. An accompanying section gives answers to the multiple-choice questions as well as suggestions for writing the essays. If you have to select a term paper topic, you may choose one from the list of suggestions in this book. This guide also provides you with a reading list, to help you when you start research for a term paper, and a selection of provocative comments by critics, to spark your thinking before you write.

THE AUTHOR
AND HIS TIMES

On a chilly April day in 1864, Henrik Ibsen arrived at the docks in the Norwegian capital of Oslo (then called Christiania). The young man was a failure. The theater he'd run had closed, and none of his own plays were successful. He had a wife and a young son to support, but all his possessions had been auctioned off two years before to pay his debts. He'd applied for a grant from his native country, Norway, but was turned down.

Disillusioned by his country and society, Ibsen, together with his wife and son, boarded a ship and left Norway, figuratively slamming the door behind him.

Fifteen years later, a similarly disillusioned Nora Helmer would slam the door on stage at the end of *A Doll's House*, helping to change the course of modern drama.

Ibsen had become disillusioned very early. In 1836, when he was eight years old, his wealthy parents went bankrupt. They were forced to move from town to a small farm. All of their old friends deserted them, and they lived for years in social disgrace. Although young Henrik appeared quiet and withdrawn, his deep, bitter anger at society would occasionally escape in the scathing caricatures he would draw or in tirades against young playmates. His sole happiness seemed to come from reading books and putting on puppet plays.

Ibsen didn't like his own family any more than he liked the "proper" society that shunned them.

His domineering father was an alcoholic, while his quiet mother found comfort in religion. This blend of overbearing husband and submissive wife makes repeated appearances in his plays, most notably in *Brand*, in *A Doll's House*, and in *Ghosts*. After he left his parents' home at sixteen in 1844, he never went back, even years later when he got word that his mother was dying.

Hoping eventually to study medicine, Ibsen became a druggist's apprentice in Grimstad, a small Norwegian village. But he still felt like an outsider, a feeling that would dog him all his life and find expression in many of his plays. (It didn't help his social standing when he fathered an illegitimate son by a servant girl ten years older than he. Some feel that it was this unwanted child that reappears in many of his plays as a lost or murdered child. In *A Doll's House*, the nursemaid gives away her illegitimate child.) But Ibsen found he wasn't alone in his contempt for those who controlled society. He became friends with a boisterous group of young artists who specialized in political satire.

By 1848, a spirit of political unrest was sweeping Europe. Rebellions against monarchy flared in many countries. This spirit of revolution was intoxicating for Ibsen and his friends. Royalty and aristocracy seemed on their way out; the people were coming into their own.

Two years later, Ibsen moved to Oslo to attend the university but failed to complete the entrance examinations. He was so caught up in politics and writing, however, that he really didn't care. After all, modern society seemed to be at a crossroads, and the world offered infinite possibilities.

But things began to go wrong. The revolutions of 1848 faltered and finally were crushed. Artists and politicians alike lost their idealism. The world of infinite possibilities didn't really exist. Years later, Ibsen would use the experiences of this period in his plays. Certain of his characters (like Nora in *A Doll's House* and Løvborg and Hedda in *Hedda Gabler*) reflect the possibility of a society where people can reach their individual potential. But these are lonely characters who must struggle against society as well as their own human failings.

Although he avoided any further active involvement in politics, Ibsen remained a nationalist. For the first time in centuries, Norway had its own government and was trying to escape the political and artistic influence of Denmark and Sweden. Authors wrote Norwegian sagas, and the Norwegian Theater was opened in Bergen. Young Ibsen became active in Norway's artistic rebirth. His first plays were filled with sweeping poetry about Vikings and political heroes. In fact, the fourteen plays Ibsen wrote between 1850 and 1873 are said to make up his Romantic Period.

Ibsen quickly forgot about being a doctor. On the merit of two plays, he became the director of the theater at Bergen, with the assignment to write one original play each year. But things did not go well for him there. Not only were his own plays failures, but he was forced to produce plays he considered mindless and unimportant—such as drawing room comedies by the contemporary French playwright Augustin Eugène Scribe. Although Ibsen ridiculed Scribe's plays, he absorbed much about their structure, known as the *pièce bien faite* (well-made play). These were tightly woven melodramas, designed primarily to entertain, to keep theatergoers on the edge of their seats. Such plays usually included a young hero and heroine, bumbling parents, and a dastardly villain. The action hinged on coincidences, misplaced letters, misunderstandings, and some kind of time limit before which everything had to work out.

There is a real art to writing a *pièce bien faite*, because there can be no unnecessary scenes or dialogue; every word and action sets up a later action. Ibsen would use this tight structure in *A Doll's House*, but he would add elements that turned an entertainment into modern drama.

In 1858, while in Bergen, Ibsen married Susannah Thoresen. Hardly a subservient wife, she helped manage his career, run his house, and screen his guests. All through his life, however, Ibsen continued to have flirtations with pretty young women (including Laura Kieler, who was the model for Nora, and Emilie Bardach, who may have had some of Hedda Gabler's traits).

Ibsen left Bergen to become the artistic director of the Norwegian theater in Oslo. The hardship of these next few years took their toll. The theater went bankrupt in 1862, and Ibsen, destitute, reportedly became involved with moneylenders, who may have provided the model for Krogstad in *A Doll's House*. Despairing, Ibsen turned to drink, and, like Eilert Løvborg in *Hedda Gabler*, he almost lost his genius to alcohol. Finally, in April 1864, he left Norway with Susannah and their son Sigurd. Over the next twenty-seven years they lived in Rome, Dresden, and Munich.

Curiously, the first play that Ibsen wrote after leaving Norway became his first Norwegian hit. And it was this play, *Brand* (1865), that finally persuaded the Norwegian government to grant Ibsen a yearly salary to support his writing.

Success changed Ibsen's life. He no longer had

to scrape for money. He was ready for his new role. He altered his wardrobe, his appearance, and even his handwriting. He consciously made himself over into the man he always thought he could be—successful, honored, sought-after.

Even though Ibsen had left Norway, he retained strong ties to the country and all but one of his plays are set there. He kept up with literary events and trends in Scandinavia. One of these events prepared him for another major change in his thinking.

In 1872 the Danish critic Georg Brandes attacked Scandinavian writers for dealing only with the past. It was time to start discussing modern problems, he said. Ibsen listened and agreed. The time was ripe for a change in world drama. In France, Alexandre Dumas, *fils* [the son], was dramatizing social ills in plays like *La Dame aux Camélias* (*Camille*); in Russia, Anton Chekhov was mourning the death of the aristocracy, and Count Leo Tolstoy was glorifying the peasants.

Even though the popular revolutions had been defeated, social change was in the air. An educated middle class was flexing its muscles. Women were beginning to question the submissive behavior they had been taught. They were now allowed to move in educated circles although seldom permitted anything beyond a rudimentary education. Often little more than decorative servants, women could not vote and had few property rights. They were expected to be passive, no matter what their true personality was. Ibsen sided with women who sought to change their traditional role.

He decided to write plays about modern people who would use contemporary, everyday language. Writing in prose instead of poetry, he turned from imaginary, romantic settings to "photograph-ically" accurate everyday settings. His first realistic prose play was *The Pillars of Society* (1877). It was a success, but some readers feel it was only prac-tice for his next play, *A Doll's House* (1879).

It's hard for us to realize just how revolutionary *A Doll's House* was. It took the form and structure of the "well-made play" but turned it from a piece of fluff into a modern tragedy. In addition, the "hero" isn't a prince or a king—or even a member of the aristocracy. Instead, it's a middle-class *woman*, who decisively rebels against her male-dominated surroundings.

A play that questioned a woman's place in so-ciety, and asserted that a woman's self was more important than her role as wife and mother, was unheard of. Government and church officials were outraged. Some people even blamed Ibsen for the rising divorce rate! When some theaters in Ger-many refused to perform the play the way it was written, Ibsen was forced to write an alternate end-ing in which the heroine's rebellion collapses.

Despite the harsh criticism of *A Doll's House*, the play became the talk of Europe. It was soon trans-lated into many languages and performed all over the world. The furor over Ibsen's realistic plays helped him to become an international figure. Some writers like Tolstoy thought Ibsen's plays too com-mon and talky; but the English author George Ber-nard Shaw considered Ibsen to be more important than Shakespeare.

No matter what individual viewers thought about its merits, in *A Doll's House*, Ibsen had developed a new kind of drama, called a "problem play" be-cause it examines modern social and moral prob-lems. The heroes and heroines of problem plays belonged to the middle or lower class, and the plays dealt with the controversial problems of modern society. This seems commonplace today, as popular entertainment has been dealing with controversial topics for years. Until Ibsen's day, however, it just wasn't done. Many of the most important plays written in our day, like *Death of a Salesman* by Arthur Miller, have their roots in the problem play.

Ibsen's Realistic Period (1877 to 1890) earned him a place as a theater giant. Not only did he introduce controversial subjects, everyday heroes, and modern language, he resurrected and modernized the "retrospective" plot, which had been popular with the ancient Greek playwrights. In a retrospective play, like *A Doll's House* and *Hedda Gabler*, the major events have taken place before the curtain goes up. The play concerns the way the characters deal with these past events.

Hedda Gabler was another innovative experiment for Ibsen. Instead of presenting a merely social problem, he painted a psychological portrait of a fascinating and self-destructive woman.

Hedda Gabler has many striking resemblances to *A Doll's House*, even though it appeared eleven years later, in 1890. In both plays, the action takes place in the drawing room. The characters include a husband and wife, the husband's friend (who completes a romantic triangle), an old school friend of the wife's, and this friend's love interest. Both wives are in a psychological crisis: Nora is not in touch with her aggressive or "male" side, while Hedda cannot bear her own femaleness. (It's interesting to note that Ibsen wrote these plays before Freud expressed his idea that everyone has both male and female components.) Nora, a member of the middle class, deals constructively with her search for self-knowledge. Her final closing of the door at the end of the play signifies that she is going out into the world, which is full of possibilities. On the other hand, Hedda Gabler, a member of the dying aristocracy, becomes destructive and predatory. Her final action is suicide.

Despite his success, Ibsen was never satisfied with his work. He felt his major characters had all failed to achieve something important, something dramatic—and he felt the same way about himself. He was in his sixties when he wrote *Hedda Gabler* and it signaled another change in his life and writing.

In 1891, after twenty-seven years of exile, Ibsen moved back to his native Norway and into his third phase of plays, called his Symbolist Period. The main characters in these plays aren't women, but spiritually defeated old men.

Ibsen had a stroke in 1900 from which he never completely recovered. But he remained an opposing force to the end. In 1906, as he was coming out of a coma, the nurse commented to his wife that he seemed a little better. "On the contrary!" Ibsen snapped. He died a few days later.

A Doll's House[*]

THE PLAY

The Plot

It's Christmas Eve. Nora Helmer, a beautiful young wife, has been out doing some last-minute shopping. When she returns, her husband Torvald immediately comes to see what his "little squirrel" has bought. They playfully act out their roles—Torvald the big, strong husband, Nora the dependent, adoring wife.

This is a happy Christmas for the Helmers and their children because Torvald has recently been appointed manager of the bank. Soon they'll be well off and won't have to scrimp. However, Torvald will still control the cash in the house, because he feels that his irresponsible Nora lets money run through her fingers, a trait she "inherited" from her father.

An old school friend, Kristine Linde, comes to visit Nora. During the conversation, Kristine reveals that she had married a wealthy man she didn't love in order to support an invalid mother. Her husband's death three years ago left her penniless and she's returned to seek work. Nora promises to speak to Torvald about a job in his bank.

[*]The following edition was used in the preparation of this guide: Henrik Ibsen, *Four Major Plays*, Vol. 1, trans. by Rolf Fjelde, Signet Classic, 1965.

Having had such a hard time herself, Kristine is scornful of Nora's easy married life until Nora describes a secret she has been concealing for many years. Early in her marriage, when Torvald became seriously ill, she secretly borrowed a large sum to finance a year-long stay in a warmer climate. Since he did not know the extent of his illness, and since, even if he had known, borrowing money would have been against his principles, she pretended the money was from her late father. Since then she has been struggling to repay the debt by economizing from her personal allowance and by secretly working at home.

The women are interrupted by the arrival of Nils Krogstad, a clerk in Torvald's bank. When Krogstad goes into the study, Dr. Rank, an old family friend, comes out. Knowing of Krogstad's reputation as a forger, Rank tells the women that Krogstad is one of those "moral invalids." Unknown to any of them, Torvald is firing Krogstad. This leaves a vacancy, and, when Torvald joins them, he agrees to give Kristine the job. Torvald, Dr. Rank, and Kristine then leave together.

As Nora is playing happily with her three young children, Krogstad reappears. It turns out that he is the one who had lent the money to Nora. He also knows that Nora not only forged her father's signature as cosigner of the loan but dated it several days after his death. Krogstad leaves after threatening to expose Nora unless he gets his job back.

Nora pleads with Torvald to reinstate Krogstad, but he refuses. She is frantic, imagining that once Krogstad reveals the truth, Torvald will himself assume the blame for the forgery and be ruined.

The next day Dr. Rank, who is suffering from a

fatal illness, comes to visit. He speaks openly of his impending death and tells Nora that he loves her. Nora is upset, not because he loves her, but because he has told her so and ruined the innocent appearance of their relationship.

The arrival of Krogstad interrupts their conversation, and Nora slips down to the kitchen to see him. He tells her he has written a letter to her husband, which explains the debt and the forgery. Then as he leaves, he drops it into the locked mailbox. In despair because Torvald has the only key to the box, Nora thinks wildly of suicide.

When Kristine learns about the forgery, she offers to intercede with Krogstad on Nora's behalf, because she and Krogstad had once been in love.

Meanwhile, Nora gets Torvald to promise to spend the rest of the evening helping her practice the tarantella—the dance she's to perform at a masquerade party the next night. Torvald sees a letter in the mailbox, but true to his promise, he ignores it and concentrates only on Nora's dance.

The next night, while the Helmers are at the party, Krogstad and Kristine meet in the Helmers' drawing room. They forgive each other's past mistakes and are reunited. Krogstad offers to ask for his letter back, unread, from Torvald, but, unexpectedly, Kristine stops him. She has had a change of heart and says he should leave the letter—Nora and Torvald must face the truth.

Torvald drags Nora away from the party the minute she finishes the dance. He is filled with desire for her and is glad when Kristine leaves. Shortly after, Dr. Rank stops by to bid a final farewell. Nora realizes he is returning home to die alone.

Overwhelmed by his feelings for Nora, Torvald

says he wishes he could save her from something dreadful. This is her cue. Nora tells him to read his mail. She is certain that now the "miracle" will happen: Torvald will nobly offer to shoulder the guilt himself. He retires to his study with the mail. Rather than see Torvald ruined, Nora throws on her shawl and starts for the hall, determined to carry out her suicide plan.

But instead, her fine illusions about her husband crumble when an outraged Torvald storms out of his study, calling her a criminal and accusing her of poisoning their home and their children. Since his reputation is at stake, he feels completely in Krogstad's power and must submit to the blackmail. Still, he insists that they must maintain the appearance of a happy family life.

Then a second letter arrives from Krogstad, dropping the charges and returning Nora's forged note. Torvald is relieved and immediately wants to return Nora to the status of pet and child. But she has seen him as he really is. She realizes that she went straight from her father's house to her husband's and has never become her own person. She has always subordinated her opinions and her identity to those who she assumed were nobler. Now she sees that both Torvald and her father were weak, and have kept her weaker only to have someone to bully.

Nora decides to leave Torvald's house to discover who she is. She says she's not fit to raise her children in the state she's in—she's been teaching them to be mindless dolls, just as she was. When Torvald asks if she'll ever return, she replies that she could only return if the greatest miracle happened and they were truly equals, truly married.

Torvald is left clinging to this hope as his wife departs, slamming the door behind her.

The Characters*

Nora Helmer

Nora is a fascinating character for actresses to play, and for you to watch. She swings between extremes: she is either very happy or suicidally depressed, comfortable or desperate, wise or naive, helpless or purposeful. You can understand this range in Nora, because she wavers between the person she pretends to be and the one she may someday become.

At the beginning of the play, Nora is still a child in many ways, listening at doors and guiltily eating forbidden sweets behind her husband's back. She has gone straight from her father's house to her husband's, bringing along her nursemaid to underline the fact that she's never grown up. She's also never developed a sense of self. She's always accepted her father's and her husband's opinions. And she's aware that Torvald would have no use for a wife who was his equal. But like many children, Nora knows how to manipulate Torvald by pouting or by performing for him.

In the end, it is the truth about her marriage that awakens Nora. Although she may suspect that Torvald is a weak, petty man, she clings to the illusion that he's strong, that he'll protect her from the consequences of her act. But at the moment of truth, he abandons her completely. She is shocked

*Spelling of the characters' names may vary according to the translation.

into reality and sees what a sham their relationship has been. She becomes aware that her father and her husband have seen her as a doll to be played with, a figure without opinion or will of her own—first a doll-child, then a doll-wife. She also realizes that she is treating her children the same way. Her whole life has been based on illusion rather than reality.

The believability of the play hinges on your accepting Nora's sudden self-awareness. Some readers feel that she has been a child so long she couldn't possibly grow up that quickly. Others feel that she is already quite wise without realizing it, and that what happens is credible. There are lines in the play that support both arguments. It's up to you to read the play and then draw your own conclusions.

There is a parallel to the story of Nora in the life of one of Ibsen's friends, a woman named Laura Kieler. She, too, secretly borrowed money to finance a trip to a warm climate for a seriously ill husband. When she had difficulty repaying the loan, she forged a note but was discovered and placed in a mental institution. Eventually, she was released and went back to her husband for her children's sake. The story outraged Ibsen, and he fictionalized it in *A Doll's House*, although rewriting the ending.

Torvald Helmer

Probably all of you know someone like Torvald. He's a straight-laced, proper man, and proud of it. At first, he seems genuinely in love with Nora, even if he does tend to nag and preach a bit. But as the play progresses, you discover more disturbing parts of his character.

Like anyone who doubts his own power, Torvald must frequently prove it. He keeps tight control over who comes to his study and whom he speaks to at work, and over everything affecting Nora. He even has the only key to their mailbox.

During the third act, you see his need for dominance increase. His fantasies always have Nora in a submissive role. He is happiest when treating her as a father would a child. This gives an incestuous tinge to their relationship, which Nora comes to realize and abhor at the end of the play.

On the other hand, Torvald is not a bad man. He is the product of his society, one who seems to fit well in the middle-class mold. It's only when he's tested that his well-ordered house of cards comes crashing down.

Some readers question the believability of Nora's love for Torvald. How could she have been blind to the obvious faults of this dull, petty man for eight years? He must have qualities that make Nora's love credible, but at the same time he must become odious enough at the end for her to break all ties and leave immediately upon discovering his true self. What kind of marriage relationship would put a premium on Torvald's good qualities?

Besides being Nora's weak and unsupportive husband, Torvald represents a "type" of thought and behavior that contrasts with Nora in several effective ways. He represents middle-class society and its rules, while Nora represents the individual. He stands for the world of men and "logical male thinking," while Nora's thinking is more intuitive and sensitive. Can you think of other ways that Torvald and Nora are compared?

In light of these comparisons, how would you

interpret Torvald's defeat at the end? Certainly at the play's start, Torvald appears to be in command in contrast to Nora's weakness. But by the end of Act Three their roles have been reversed: he is the weak one, begging for another chance, and Nora has found strength. Does the author mean to suggest that the ideas of male supremacy and middle-class respectability were changing?

Dr. Rank

Dr. Rank is an old family friend, whose relationship to the Helmers is deeper than it appears. He always visits with Torvald first, but it is Nora he really comes to see. Both Rank and Nora prefer each other's company to Torvald's.

Although Nora flirts with Rank and fantasizes about a rich gentleman dying and leaving her everything, she never acknowledges her true feelings—the attraction she feels for older, father-figures. Rank at least is honest in declaring his love for Nora.

The doctor serves several important functions in the play. His physical illness, inherited from his loose-living father, parallels the "moral illness" shared by Krogstad and Nora. The hereditary nature of Rank's disease, although it is never identified, suggests the possibility of immorality passing from generation to generation. Rank's concern with appearing normal despite his illness parallels Torvald's concerns with maintaining the appearance of a normal marriage after he discovers Nora's moral "disease."

Dr. Rank helps Nora on her journey to self-discovery. He forces her to face the reality of his death, which prepares her for the death of her marriage. He also forces her to look behind appearances to see the romantic nature of her and Rank's relationship. Nora refuses to deal with both of these issues in the second act, but by the third act she and Rank are through with masquerades and are both openly preparing to die. At the end, Rank realizes and accepts his approaching death, while Nora realizes and accepts the death of her marriage.

Kristine Linde

Mrs. Linde, Nora's old friend, is the first "voice from the past" who affects the future. On the one hand, she is like Nora because she's gone through what Nora is about to face. Kristine has come out of a marriage that was socially acceptable and emotionally bankrupt. On the other hand, she is different from Nora because, having already been disillusioned, she has now gained a firm grasp on reality. She has hope, but it's based on knowing and accepting the truth about herself and about Krogstad. Kristine is the first to see Nora's marriage for the pretense it is. It is Kristine who decides, for better or worse, that Torvald has to know the whole truth about Nora's forgery.

Kristine and Krogstad's compassionate and realistic relationship contrasts with Nora and Torvald's playacting. While the Helmers' socially acceptable relationship crumbles because it's based on deceptions, Nils and Kristine's relationship is renewed and strengthened because it's based on truth.

Nils Krogstad

Nils Krogstad, a clerk in Helmer's bank, is called immoral by several other characters in the play, but is he? We usually think of an immoral person as someone who has no regard for right and wrong.

But Krogstad *is* concerned with right and wrong. He's also concerned about his reputation and its effect on his children. Although he has been a forger, he wants to reform and tries desperately to keep his job and social standing. Once they're lost, he decides to play the part of the villain in which society has imprisoned him. His attempt to blackmail Nora sets the play's action in motion.

Through his blackmail letter he forces Nora into self-knowledge. He also affects some of the other characters in ways that reveal not only the truth about him, but the truth about them as well. For example, you discover much of Torvald's pettiness from the way he reacts to Krogstad as an inferior. Despite his superficial role as a villain, Krogstad understands himself and the world. Although some find his conversion in Act Three hard to believe, he (together with Kristine) offers that message of hope that gives promise to Nora's future.

Other Elements
SETTING

A Doll's House takes place in a large Norwegian town. The entire drama unfolds on one set, a "comfortable room" in the Helmers' house that serves both as a drawing room in which to receive guests and as a family room where the children play and where the family sets up its Christmas tree. There is a door to the entryway and another to Torvald's study.

Ibsen describes this setting in minute detail. About midway through his career, he adapted a style of drama that has been called "photographic." Instead of creating various country or city scenes as background for his characters, he "takes a picture" of one room they inhabit. Every piece of furniture, every prop reveals the character of the people who live in this place. For example, in the Helmers' drawing room there is a "small bookcase with richly bound books." What better way to describe Torvald, their owner, than as "richly bound"—someone who looks good from the outside? Also, the Christmas tree serves to represent various stages in Nora Helmer's life. When her life appears happy, the tree is beautifully trimmed. When her happiness is shattered, the tree is stripped and drooping. Ibsen has described the set and its props precisely, so that every production will reproduce this same "photograph" of the Helmers' living room.

Probably the most significant thing about the setting of this play is that it concerns middle-class characters and values. It takes place in an unnamed city, where banking and law would be considered normal and respectable occupations. Banking is the occupation most closely associated with money, the symbol of middle-class goals, and the crimes of the characters—Nora, her father, and Krogstad—are monetary ones. Notice also how Torvald, a lawyer and bank manager, is preoccupied with Nora's extravagance, or waste of money.

Up until Ibsen's time, serious drama had been almost exclusively concerned with members of the aristocracy or military heroes. Comedy had served to depict the lives of the farmers, workers, and lower class. But *A Doll's House* is a serious drama about the middle class. Some might even say it is a tragedy of everyday life. In light of today's understanding of marital roles and the larger issue of women's self-awareness, would you call the fate of the Helmers' marriage a tragedy?

THEMES

The major themes of *A Doll's House* recur in many of Ibsen's plays, including *Hedda Gabler*.

1. THE INDIVIDUAL AND SOCIETY

Ibsen felt strongly that society should reflect people's needs, not work against them. In *A Doll's House*, society's rules prevent the characters from seeing and expressing their true nature. When Krogstad tells Nora that the law takes no account of good motives, she cries, "Then they must be very bad laws!"

At the end of the play, she realizes she has existed in two households ruled by men and has accepted the church and society without ever questioning these institutions. In the third act, Nora separates herself from the "majority" and the books that support them. "But," she says, "I can't go on believing what the majority says, or what's written in books. I have to think over these things myself and try to understand them." The individual has triumphed over society, but at a heavy price that includes her children. When Nora walks out the door, she becomes a social outcast.

2. DUTY TO ONESELF

Ibsen seems to be saying that your greatest duty is to understand yourself. At the beginning of the play, Nora doesn't realize she has a self. She's playing a role. The purpose of her life is to please Torvald or her father, and to raise her children. But by the end of the play, she discovers that her "most sacred duty" is to herself. She leaves to find out who she is and what she thinks.

3. THE PLACE OF WOMEN

This was a major theme in late nineteenth-century literature and appeared in Leo Tolstoy's *Anna*

Karenina, Gustave Flaubert's *Madame Bovary*, and Thomas Hardy's *Tess of the D'Urbervilles*, to name only a few.

Ibsen refused to be called a feminist, preferring to be known as a humanist. He had little patience with people, male or female, who didn't stand up for their rights and opinions.

Still, he argued that society's rules came from the traditionally male way of thinking. He saw the woman's world as one of human values, feelings, and personal relationships, while men dealt in the abstract realm of laws, legal rights, and duties. In *A Doll's House*, Nora can't really see how it is wrong to forge a name in order to save a life, but Torvald would rather die than break the law or borrow money. This difference in thinking is what traps Nora.

However, for Ibsen, the triumph of the individual embraces the right of women to express themselves. In the end, Nora's duty to know herself is more important than her female role.

4. APPEARANCE AND REALITY

At the beginning of the play, family life is not what it seems. Nora is Torvald's "little squirrel"; they appear to have a perfect marriage and their home is debt-free. Nora seems content and Torvald is in control. Scandal can't touch them. Everyone concerned wants to keep up appearances. But, little by little, as the play progresses, reality replaces appearances.

Nora is upset when Dr. Rank shatters the appearance that their relationship is innocent. Torvald insists on keeping up the appearance of marriage even after rejecting Nora for her past crime. He is appalled when Krogstad calls him by his first name at the bank—it doesn't appear proper. Dr. Rank wants to appear healthy. Krogstad and Nora want to hide their deeds and are enmeshed in a tissue of lies.

Only when the characters give up their deceptions and cast off their elaborately constructed secrets can they be whole. Ask yourself how all the characters achieve this freedom from appearances by the play's end. Do any of them fail?

5. THE COLLAPSE OF THE PARENTAL IDEAL

Nora seems to be under the impression that her father was perfect, and she tried to replace him—first with Torvald, then with Rank. When she realizes her father wasn't looking out for her best interests, it's only a short step to discovering that Torvald isn't either.

STYLE

After finishing an earlier play, Ibsen wrote a letter saying, "We are no longer living in the age of Shakespeare . . . what I desired to depict were human beings, and therefore I would not let them talk the language of the gods." This doesn't seem unusual to us today because we expect the major characters in contemporary plays and movies to speak in everyday language. But in Ibsen's day the use of common speech was shocking. Writers in the mid-1800s were largely devoted to the tradition requiring plays to be about larger-than-life heroes who spoke grand and noble language. Even Ibsen's early plays were about heroic events and contained dialogue filled with poetry.

But later he wanted to do something different.

He wanted to write realistic plays about the average middle-class people who made up his audience and who spoke the way they did. In *A Doll's House*, the characters use everyday vocabulary and colloquial expressions. They interrupt each other, correct themselves, and speak in incomplete sentences. This switch to realistic dialogue is considered one of the major breakthroughs in the development of modern drama.

It's also important to note that Ibsen was writing in Dano-Norwegian. For centuries, Norway's art and literature had been heavily influenced by Denmark. Even when a group of authors finally started a Norwegian writers' society, they met in Denmark. Then in the 1800s, Norwegians became very nationalistic. They wanted their own art and their own language. In those days there were only two languages to choose from: a mixture of peasant dialects or a refined mixture of Norwegian and Danish. Ibsen was part of the first generation who had grown up speaking and writing Dano-Norwegian. (Today in Norway, even Ibsen's language sounds old-fashioned and stilted because the language has reduced the amount of Danish and increased the amount of colloquial Norwegian.)

There are several notable differences between Ibsen's original language and English translations. English has many synonyms and uses many modifiers. Dano-Norwegian, on the other hand, tends to be simpler, using fewer words and adjectives. It will use a few very brief, strong images, instead of effusive descriptions. This is evident in *A Doll's House* in several ways. There are very few metaphors (elaborate word comparisons) or descriptive adjectives. The sparse language lends itself to understatement and to multilevel meanings for single words. Much of the humor comes from understanding the layers of different meaning.

Ibsen adds his own strict control of language to this natural Norwegian economy. None of the dialogue is superfluous; it is all packed with meaning. In fact, often the dialogue means more than the character knows it means! An example of this "loaded" dialogue occurs when Torvald talks about how an immoral parent poisons the whole family. He is referring to Krogstad, but Nora's replies refer to herself.

The differences between English and Norwegian make Ibsen's plays somewhat difficult to translate. Ibsen's own wish was "that the dialogue in the translations be kept as close to everyday, ordinary speech as possible." One difficulty, for example, is that Norwegian doesn't use contractions, but English without contractions sounds dry and stilted. Most modern translators try to keep Ibsen's text close to everyday English and the spirit, if not the word, of the original. This means that phrases may change from earlier to later translations depending on current usage. Also, be aware that some versions available in America are British and use distinctly British speech patterns.

FORM AND STRUCTURE

The basic form for *A Doll's House* comes from the French *pièce bien faite* (well-made play), with which Ibsen became familiar while producing plays in Oslo and Bergen, Norway. At the time, France was the leader in world drama; however, "serious" dramatists in France looked down on the *pièce bien faite* as low-class entertainment. Typically, this kind of play contained the same stock characters—including the domineering father, the innocent woman in distress, the jealous husband, the loyal friend, the cruel villain—who underwent predictable crises involving lost letters, guilty secrets, and mistaken identity. Intrigue and tension-building delays were heaped on top of each other until the final embrace or pistol shot. There was always a moral to the story.

Ibsen adopted the techniques but changed the characters. Instead of being cardboard types, they are complicated people whose problems the audience can identify with. You (as the reader or audience member) can learn something about your-

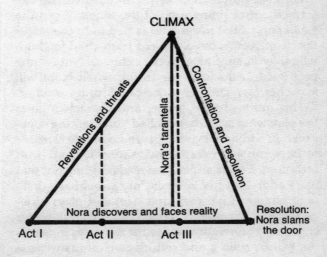

self and your world through the intrigue and tension
onstage. Nora's plight makes you consider your
own ideas and relationships, for example.

Another structural technique commonly used by
Ibsen is to place all of the important "events" *before*
the play opens. Instead of witnessing the events
as they occur, you find them revealed and ex-
plained in different ways as the play progresses.
The key past event in this play is Nora's secret loan
obtained by forging her father's signature. Other
important past events are Krogstad's crime, Mrs.
Linde's marriage, and Dr. Rank's inherited fatal
illness.

The action of the play is very compressed. It
takes place in one location (the living room) over
a period of three days. The five major characters
are closely related, and their lives and roles mirror
or contrast with each other's. One character cannot
act without affecting each of the others. Even the
small part of the nursemaid is tied in to the major
theme of Nora's development from child to child-
wife to woman. She not only connects Nora to the
past but foreshadows the future when Nora will
leave her own children to be cared for by another.

This unity of time, place, and characters gives
the play what some have called "unrelenting cohesion." In addition, every prop and costume is meant
to be symbolic, every conversation layered with
meanings. For example, one reader points out that
Nora addresses her baby as "my sweet baby doll"
(a reminder of her own doll role) and plays hide-
and-seek (a reminder of hidden truth) with the older
children. You might want to list the ways in which
the words, action, and setting give off many messages.

Just as the details reveal the meaning, the overall action is constructed to make you feel the tension mounting within the play. Act One proceeds from the calm of everyday life to disturbing interruptions and revelations. In Act Two, thoughts of death and suicide culminate in the climax of Nora's frantic tarantella. In Act Three, you feel the calm as the confrontation between Nora and Torvald approaches. Some think that the play's resolution—Nora's decision to depart—is also its true climax.

The Story
ACT ONE

It's Christmas Eve at the Helmers' house, and a warm fire crackles against the cold winter day outside. Nora Helmer, a beautiful young wife and mother, happily comes home with her arms full of presents. She puts the packages on a table and gives a generous tip to the delivery boy who's brought the Christmas tree. Then she tells the maid to keep the tree hidden from the children and hums to herself as she guiltily nibbles on macaroons, her favorite snack. We're immediately caught up in the surprises and planning that surround Christmas.

NOTE: Ibsen's stage description of the Helmers' drawing room is unusually precise and detailed. You'll find that this fits in perfectly. The play is so carefully planned that every prop serves a function. Already we know the home fire is burning, and we'll soon see that, by eating macaroons, Nora is playing with fire. Her first word, "hide," portends that the appearance of a happy home is just that: an appearance. Many things besides the tree are hidden from view.

Nora "steals" over to listen at her husband's study door, much the way a child might sneak around a grown-up. Torvald's first words to her, "Is that my little lark twittering . . . my squirrel rummaging . . . ?" could be a father's to a small daughter. But if she's treated like a child or a pet, she's an *adored* one. Torvald is genuinely glad to see her, and he comes from his study to talk to her and see what she's bought. Nora seems to be content with this relationship. From the beginning she manipulates her husband with the same ingenious plots that children use to get their way. She pleads and pouts and flirts, and bolsters his ego by chiming "Whatever you say, Torvald," and "You know I could never think of going against you."

NOTE: This dominant husband/submissive wife relationship represented the ideal for many middle-class Europeans who first saw this play. But recognizing their own type of behavior at the beginning of the play made the ending seem a personal insult. How do you view Nora and Torvald from this early exchange between the two?

Ask yourself how you feel about relationships between men and women. Is there always some kind of role-playing going on? If so, what kinds of roles seem to fulfill women? to fulfill men? Are roles necessary? As you read the play, try to figure out how Ibsen would answer these questions.

Despite their playfulness, Nora and Torvald are speaking about a serious subject: money. Torvald is sure that Nora has a woman's understanding of money—that is, she can't handle it properly. Thus, all the finances in this household are attended to by him, and when Nora wants money she must wheedle it out of him. Now she wants him to borrow money for Christmas gifts. Even though he has just been made manager of the bank and they won't have to worry about money, Torvald doesn't want to owe anyone anything, even for a month, for then a bit of "freedom's lost." This question of borrowing foreshadows the revelation of Nora's great secret of the past. When it is revealed, think back to how she might be reacting now to this lecture about debt.

Still he rewards Nora's pout with money and condescendingly lays the blame for her alleged mismanagement on heredity. According to Torvald, Nora's father let money carelessly run through his fingers in the same way.

NOTE: Heredity   This is a favorite theme of Ibsen's. His next play, *Ghosts*, deals with a fatal illness that is inherited by a son because of his father's sexual activities.

Throughout this play, heredity will be credited for passing on physical traits or problems (like brown hair or Dr. Rank's disease) from parent to child. Heredity will also be blamed for passing along moral traits like Krogstad's dishonesty and Nora's mismanagement of money. But Ibsen wants you to wonder how much of moral character results from heredity and how much results from environment. Is character determined by genes or by what you're taught? What are the consequences if character is something you're born with? How is the situation different if it's something you learn? Be on the lookout for how each character views heredity. Who is proven wrong?

Torvald suspects Nora has been eating macaroons, another extravagance of which he disapproves. She repeatedly denies it. You now have a clear picture of the control Torvald exercises and his way of thinking. Borrowing money or eating sweets is forbidden in the Helmer house. Nora is adorable and impractical, and money runs through her fingers. But there is one flaw in this picture: Nora has lied about the macaroons. It's a small thing which seems to fit into their domestic games. You will soon become aware of how important lies have been in their married life. Almost immediately after presenting this picture of typical middle-class married life, Ibsen will take you beneath the surface. Past truths will be exposed to challenge this marriage.

The first voice from the past to disturb the comfortable present is that of Nora's old school friend Kristine, now Mrs. Linde, a widow who has just returned to town. The Helmers' friend Dr. Rank comes in at the same time. The men go into the study, leaving the women to talk. At first Nora acts the same way with Kristine as she had acted with Torvald, continuing her pleasant, empty-headed chatter. But instead of being manipulated by it, Kristine treats Nora with pity and subtle insults. Kristine has been through years of hardship. She married a man she didn't love because she needed money to care for her ailing mother. Since then, both her husband and her mother have died. Kristine is now alone, trying to support herself. She assumes, justifiably, that Nora has been coddled and protected all her life. There is no sign in Nora's childlike behavior up to this point that she's ever faced hardship. The need for money and the way men in an earlier era controlled it at the expense of women is again being raised. As you read, keep in mind the role of money and the way women had traditionally obtained it.

NOTE: Kristine's description of her empty marriage, of how her husband left her nothing, not even children or "a sense of loss to feed on," is beyond Nora's comprehension. Here is another foreshadowing, this time of how completely Nora's attitude toward Torvald and marriage will change in two days' time.

Nora at once plans to help Kristine get a job in Torvald's bank. She boasts about how she'll arrange it by manipulating Torvald. Kristine thinks her offer of help is very kind, especially since Nora has no concept of life's burdens.

Can you remember a time you've been indignant with someone for passing judgment on you when that person didn't even know all the facts? That's exactly how Nora feels when Kristine, who should be her equal, treats her like a sheltered child. She's annoyed enough to tell Kristine her biggest secret—the key "event" of the play, even though it has already taken place. Like Kristine, who has made a sacrifice for her mother, Nora, too, has sacrificed for someone. Near the beginning of her marriage, Torvald became very ill and might have died if he hadn't traveled south to a milder climate. Knowing that Torvald's principles would never have allowed him to borrow money for the trip, Nora herself secretly arranged for a large sum from a moneylender and pretended it came from her father, who had recently died. For seven years she's scrimped and saved to pay off the loan. In fact, far from being a spendthrift, she has been economizing by making her own Christmas decorations and by secretly copying documents to raise money!

Now, with Torvald's new position, she'll be able to pay off the remainder of the debt and bury her secret.

NOTE: It now seems that Nora's relationship with Torvald is guided by keeping secrets. What is the necessity of secrets? Keep a count of the various secrets of each character as the play progresses. How do they affect each life? How are they revealed? When does secret information give power? When is it a burden?

We get an even more intimate picture of Nora and Torvald's marriage. Kristine asks if Nora will ever tell Torvald what she's done, and Nora responds no! "How painfully humiliating for him if he ever found out he was in debt to me. That would just ruin our relationship. Our beautiful happy home would never be the same."

NOTE: Knowing and Realizing Nora is absolutely right. But although she *knows*, she doesn't yet *realize* what a petty man Torvald is. She knows their relationship is completely one-sided—Torvald keeps her in constant debt to him. Any sign of strength from her would ruin their relationship. But she has a hunch she might need the power over Torvald that this secret will give her, "when he stops enjoying my dancing and dressing up and reciting for him." Nora already knows more about their relationship than she thinks she does, but she hasn't ever been forced to consciously face these facts. What is the practical difference between knowing something and realizing it? Would Nora behave the same way if she truly realized what kind of man Torvald is?

It might seem a little odd that Nora talks so openly to a woman like Kristine who's so different from her, and whom she hasn't seen in ten years. But once she's confided her splendid secret, Nora goes on to talk of her fantasies—including one in which a wealthy old man falls in love with her and leaves her his money when he dies.

NOTE: This fantasy serves two purposes: it underscores Nora's "father fixation" for older men, and it announces Dr. Rank's appearance. Watch for the significance of this fantasy in Nora and Rank's relationship.

No sooner has Nora finished describing her little Eden than the serpent enters the garden in the form of Mr. Krogstad. Both women react uneasily to his presence. Mrs. Linde turns away and looks out the window, and Nora nervously asks why he wants to see Torvald. Krogstad, who works in Torvald's bank, assures Nora it's "dry business." As Krogstad goes in to see Torvald, Dr. Rank comes out of the study to join the women.

The first thing we learn about Dr. Rank is that he is terminally ill. He compares himself to Krogstad, who is "morally sick." Watch for the theme of inherited moral defects as the play progresses.

In a mood of nervous gaiety, Nora throws caution to the wind by breaking one of Torvald's rules—she offers her guests the forbidden macaroons. But the minute Torvald appears, she hides the macaroons. Through flattery and exaggeration, she manages to get Kristine a job in Torvald's bank.

Krogstad has already gone. Rank and Torvald then leave with Kristine, who is off to find an apartment.

As they are going, Nora's three children come running in from outside with their nurse. Nora immediately drops everything to play with them. Symbolically, she calls the youngest her "sweet little doll baby" and joins them in a game of hide-and-seek. Doesn't this remind you of Nora's "doll" status with Torvald and the "games" they play together? Not surprisingly, Nora is the one who hides. Also not surprisingly, as you will learn, Krogstad is the one who returns to catch her playing her game. He alone knows the game she's been playing all these years.

NOTE: The fact that Ibsen chooses to bring the children on stage means he wants you to see them and hear them. They must be real to the audience, because they'll figure prominently in Nora's future thoughts and actions. It is also a chance for you to see Nora as a conventional nineteenth-century mother, just as you have seen her as a conventional wife.

Nora sends the children to their nurse and faces Krogstad alone. He reveals that he used to know Kristine Linde, and that the job she was just promised is his job—Torvald is firing him. We also discover another secret—Krogstad is the moneylender that Nora is paying back. He threatens to tell Torvald about the loan unless Nora gets him his job back. This job is vitally important to him, because it means respectability for the sake of his young sons. What does this suggest about Krogstad's view of transferable morality?

Nora insists she can't help him and dares him to reveal her debt. It would only cause a little unpleasantness for her, and Torvald would then surely fire him. But Krogstad holds the cards this time. Nora, being a woman, could not have gotten the loan on her own credit. In fact, Nora had forged her father's name but dated the signature several days after her father's death. Nora has committed a serious crime, forgery—the same crime that marred Krogstad's reputation and has continued to haunt him.

NOTE: In order to emphasize his ideas, Ibsen creates very close parallels between his characters. Notice how Krogstad's desire for respectability echoes Torvald's position. His plea on behalf of his children is no different, it seems, from Nora's pleas on behalf of hers. The identical nature of their crimes is not a coincidence. How do you react to this type of repetition? Does it seem unrealistic? Does it help you see what Ibsen's message is? Do you understand the characters better?

Nora cries that their crimes weren't similar at all. Her motives had been pure, to save a life, while his motives had been for selfish gain. He calmly points out that "Laws don't inquire into motives." Nora thinks "they must be very poor laws."

NOTE: There are other instances in the play where a woman stands for individuality against a male-oriented society. Here, Krogstad emphasizes that society is much more concerned with the letter of the law than with individual intent. How do society's impersonal rules and laws conflict with each character's specific needs? What does this play say about the resolution of this conflict? Which is more important—individual fulfillment or society's demands?

Krogstad's blackmail is complete. If he loses his job and respectability, he will drag Nora down with him. He leaves a stunned and disbelieving Nora behind. She simply can't comprehend that a person can be indicted for a crime committed out of love. Nora is shaken but returns to her usual techniques to keep reality at arm's length. Torvald returns, asking if someone was just there. Nora lies again, but to no avail. Torvald saw Krogstad leaving. He guesses the clerk's purpose and is angered by Nora's request that Krogstad be reinstated.

A discussion of Krogstad's—and by implication, Nora's—crime follows. It condemns her utterly. Like the law, Torvald has no interest in motives, either. A person who's committed forgery has to put on a false face even in family circles, says Torvald. Furthermore, dishonesty that turns up so early in life is usually caused by a lying mother! The theme of moral sickness returns.

When he leaves, Nora is clearly shaken by his attitude. The children beg her to play, but she refuses to let them near her. Is she a moral invalid? The question terrifies her. "Hurt my children? Poison my home" she cries. "That's not true. Never. Never in all the world." Her values remain intact. Home and family are her first priorities.

How is Nora likely to respond to Krogstad's threat at this point? How would you respond? Why is your answer likely to be different from Nora's? Is there any "right" way out of the situation?

NOTE: By now, you will have noticed that all the important dramatic events in Nora's life took place *before* the play started: the forgery, the borrowed money, the trip to save Torvald's life. The first act has served to reveal a situation that already exists. Krogstad's attempt to dislodge and reveal the past sets the action of Acts Two and Three in motion. From now on, coincidence and the characters' responses to their current situations will determine the play's resolution.

ACT TWO

Christmas Eve has turned into Christmas Day. After the presents and excitement, the symbolic tree has been stripped and the candles are burned out. For everyone else, the waiting is over, but for Nora it's just beginning.

In the first act, Torvald called her a squirrel and a bird; now she paces like an animal that's newly aware of its cage. She's trying to convince herself that Krogstad won't carry out his threat, but nevertheless she checks the mailbox and listens fearfully for visitors.

Anne-Marie, the nursemaid, enters. The short dialogue that follows between Nora and Anne-Marie serves three important functions:

1.   It tells us that Anne-Marie was Nora's own nursemaid. This underscores the fact that Nora went straight from her father's "nursery" to Torvald's home, without having to grow up.

2.   It reveals that Anne-Marie had to give up her own illegitimate daughter to nurse Nora. Nora knows that she might be in a parallel situation, forced to give up her children for their own good.

3.   It establishes that Anne-Marie will be there to "mother" the children even if Nora isn't.

NOTE: In the conversation between Nora and Anne-Marie, you can see how Ibsen "loads" his dialogue with additional meanings. For example, Nora responds not only to what Anne-Marie says, but to what she might be implying about Nora's current predicament. Where else in the play have you seen characters in the same discussion talking about two completely different things? How could this be related to the pattern of secrets?

When Kristine Linde arrives, Nora begins to discuss with her Dr. Rank and his "inherited" illness. Nora suggests that his fatal illness (possibly syphilis) is the result of his father's sexual escapades. Again, Ibsen connects two generations with a moral taint. Later on, the old doctor expresses the idea that sometimes one family member must suffer for the sins of another.

NOTE: Ibsen wrote his plays before Sigmund Freud advanced his theories about our conscious and subconscious being influenced by our parents and our childhood experiences. But notice in this play how frequently what the characters do and say is attributed to the fact they have been conditioned physically and morally by past events beyond their control. Ibsen calls this influence heredity, but how would you characterize it?

Kristine recognizes and reveals to Nora the sexual component of Nora's relationship with Rank, and connects Rank with Nora's earlier fantasy about a rich admirer. (The sexual longings for a parent figure also play a large part in Freud's teachings.)

When Torvald returns home, Kristine goes off to repair Nora's peasant-girl outfit for the costume party. Torvald unwittingly continues the heredity theme by reminding Nora that her father wasn't above reproach in the business world.

Nora again pleads on Krogstad's behalf, and Torvald's replies are even more revealing. He doesn't mind that Nora is trying to influence him, but he minds very much that it would *appear* that way to others. To him, appearance and reputation are everything. He even admits that it isn't Krogstad's moral failings that bother him. It's that Krogstad is an old boyhood friend who has the nerve to call him by his first name in front of everyone at the bank!

Even Nora recognizes these as petty concerns. When she says so, Torvald feels threatened and insulted. To prove his "power," he immediately sends the letter of dismissal to Krogstad.

Then Torvald forgives Nora and assures her that whatever comes, he'll bear "the whole weight" of it for both of them. Nora thinks he'll take the penalty of her forgery upon himself should it be revealed. As Torvald leaves, she's frantic. She can't let her crime ruin her husband—she's got to find an escape! The stage directions here suggest impending doom: *"During the following scene, it begins getting dark."*

Dr. Rank enters with news of a sad discovery. Nora, in her anxious state, is so sure he's discovered her crime that she's almost relieved at his real discovery—he doesn't have long to live. In this scene, Dr. Rank forces Nora along her path to adulthood. He tries to make her confront two things: his impending death and his love for her. Like a child, she calls him "naughty" for bringing up indelicate subjects and refuses to discuss them. At this point Nora, like Torvald, is concerned with appearances. She doesn't mind that Dr. Rank loves her, but, as a married woman, she minds very much that he improperly brings the subject out into the open.

NOTE: Even though Nora's secrets are beginning to be revealed, she still refuses to deal with them.

She was about to ask Rank for help and advice when he proclaimed his love. By refusing to deal with his feelings for her, and possibly her own for him, she loses both her chance for his help and her cherished fantasy about a secret lover's will.

Rank unwittingly alarms Nora by the implications of two statements he makes: "To suffer . . . for somebody else's sins . . . in every single family, in some way or another, this inevitable retribution of nature goes on." He adds that people who "go away" are soon forgotten. The doctor is talking about himself and his father's disease, and his own approaching death, but Nora is thinking about her own past and her own future. Not wanting Torvald to suffer for her sins, she thinks of suicide as an escape.

Nora's level of awareness about herself, her surroundings, and her relationships is becoming an issue. When Rank asks her point-blank if she's known about his love for her, she answers, "Oh, how can I tell what I know or don't know? . . . Why did you have to be so clumsy, Dr. Rank! Everything was so good." Nora is experiencing doubt, an uncomfortable emotion, but necessary as a prelude to self-knowledge.

The arrival of Krogstad puts even more pressure on Nora. Krogstad is especially dangerous because he understands Torvald's pettiness and Nora's fears. In fact, he's the first character who's been able to read Nora's hidden thoughts. He knows she's considered running away or even committing suicide. He explains that he had the same thoughts himself, when his forgery was discovered. But he knows she doesn't have the courage to die any more than he did.

Krogstad is as desperate as Nora and acts ruthlessly to gain his ends. Suicide won't solve anything, he says, because he can bring scandal on her family even after she's dead. He then enlarges his blackmail demands. Having his old job back isn't good enough; he wants a better position, and eventually to be Torvald's right-hand man. Krogstad correctly guesses that once Torvald knows the truth, he'll do anything to save his precious reputation.

On his way out, Krogstad puts the letter damning Nora into the mailbox. A time bomb has been dropped. Can you imagine a household nowadays where only the husband has a key to the mailbox? Nora can only stare through the glass at the deadly letter in horror. But, at the same time, her fantasy timetable is set in motion. First "the miracle" will happen—Torvald will find out about her crime; then he'll take the blame on himself. Nora can never allow this. She'll commit suicide in order to take all the responsibility on herself. Notice how the central point in this scene is the assumption that Torvald will shoulder the burden of guilt. Is Nora contemplating suicide out of love? out of deference to society's demands? as a point of honor? or out of fear of Torvald's response? Can you find evidence in the text to support one or more of these reasons?

Kristine reenters, and each woman discovers the other's secret. When Kristine realizes that Krogstad is the moneylender, she reveals that she and Krogstad were once in love. Kristine leaves at once to persuade him to ask Torvald to return the letter unopened.

Torvald and Rank come out of the study.

NOTE: Stagecraft Here, Ibsen makes heavy use of *dramatic irony*. Dramatic irony occurs when you, as the reader or audience member, have more information than the characters do, and this information adds more meaning to the lines than the characters realize. A prime example is Torvald's entrance line: "Rank had me expecting some grand masquerade." He's disappointed not to find Nora dressed up in her party costume, but you know he's watching a real masquerade.

Nora tells him she needs so much help on her dance for the party that he must promise not to do any more business that evening. She takes on her adoring, dependent role so effectively that Torvald promises to spend the whole evening reteaching her the tarantella they learned in Italy. Nora dances in a frenzy, as if her "life were at stake." Fittingly, the fatally ill Dr. Rank joins in this violent dance of death by accompanying Nora at the piano. Kristine enters and stands dumbfounded at the door.

NOTE: This scene is echoed in the second play in this guide, *Hedda Gabler*. Hedda plays wildly on her piano before her suicide.

Torvald gets Nora to admit there's a letter from Krogstad in the box but keeps his promise not to open any mail until "tomorrow night, after you've danced."

"Then you'll be free," Nora assures him. In the meantime, she orders the last meal of a condemned woman: champagne till daybreak and heaps of macaroons.

When Torvald and Dr. Rank leave, Kristine informs Nora that Krogstad has left town until the next night. Nora says it's just as well: "the miracle" must happen. In light of Nora's insistence that Torvald will act honorably, ask yourself why she even waits for him to open the letter before killing herself. Is it because she isn't truly convinced? Is she giving herself time to reconsider? Or has Krogstad convinced her that suicide wouldn't help? "Thirty-one hours to live," she says. Then "the little lark" goes in to join Torvald and the others at dinner.

Meanwhile, the letter "bomb" is ticking away, waiting to explode in Act Three. Then Nora will have to face, not only the exposure of her crime, but the meaning of her life.

ACT THREE

Nora's waiting is almost over. It's the next night, and she's upstairs at the party, about to dance the tarantella. But instead of watching Nora's performance, you're downstairs in the Helmers' drawing room with Mrs. Linde. She's waiting for Krogstad to arrive in response to her note.

NOTE: Some readers find it hard to believe that Kristine would ask Krogstad to meet her at the

Helmers' house, given the explosive situation. Krogstad wonders why himself. True, it wouldn't be proper to meet at Kristine's, and she needs to talk to him in private. The most important reason, of course, is Ibsen's need to maintain "unity of place"—a one-room setting for the whole story. As with some other situations in the play that may seem hard to accept as believable, Ibsen often sacrifices realism to the demands of an intense theatrical presentation. Think of the "coincidence" of the double forgeries, the giving of Krogstad's position in the bank to Kristine, and the nursemaid's former renunciation of her own child.

Kristine admits that she's always loved Krogstad. She married her first husband only for his money. Krogstad doesn't think that's an acceptable excuse, and Kristine doesn't argue. When Krogstad lost Kristine, "it was as if the solid ground dissolved" from under his feet.

Kristine offers him help. He assumes "help" means she'll step aside so he can have his job back. But she's realistic. She knows that even if she resigned, Torvald wouldn't reinstate him. The help she means is her love. She offers to marry him and help raise his children. Krogstad assumes she won't love him when she knows his past and his reputation. But she does know and forgives him completely. Why does Ibsen again stretch the story's credibility by reuniting these former lovers, with the connecting links of Nora and the bank? What important messages about love, respectability, and guilty secrets are being clearly presented by this coincidental situation?

The two couples have traded places. Nora and

Torvald, who seemed at first a happy couple, are being pushed apart by secrets and lies. Krogstad and Kristine, who had been separated by dishonesty, are willing to face their past mistakes. Their love, apparently dead, is revived. Does this reversal give you a hint about the fate of Nora and Torvald?

Some readers find Krogstad's reformation as a result of Kristine's compassion too quick and easy to be believable. Others feel that he's been a basically good man all along, caught in a downward spiral. Either way, their story is completed. The future awaits them and now it is time to let the Helmers' fate be decided. Nora's tarantella is heard upstairs. The Helmers will soon return.

NOTE: In the first act, Ibsen used theatrical devices and revelations of past events to begin the story. Then, a number of coincidences caused confrontations. But from here through the rest of the play, the action is determined solely by character— how people respond to situations and interact with each other. The resolution of the major conflict will fall squarely on Nora and Torvald.

Kristine and Krogstad still have a part in the Helmers' predicament. The first major action based on character occurs when Krogstad offers to ask for his letter back. Kristine unexpectedly tells him not to. She feels that the deception between Nora and Torvald should not go on. Is Kristine right in deciding that it's better for Torvald to know? Is it her business to make this decision at all? Should a person tell the truth at all costs? This is a question that Ibsen asks in several of his plays. The cost of truth to Nora and Torvald will be high. Whether too high, you will have to decide.

Nora and Torvald return home from the party to find Kristine there. Torvald describes Nora's successful performance but, as you might expect, thinks it was lacking in respectability, a little too wild and emotional.

NOTE: Notice Helmer's critique of Nora's dance. "She . . . got a tumultuous hand—which was well earned, although the performance may have been a bit too naturalistic—I mean it rather overstepped the proprieties of art." Ibsen is indulging in a bit of inside humor here since this is a criticism that was often made of his own plays.

In the same speech, Torvald utters the play's grandest irony, but one that you won't understand until the curtain goes down. He says, "An exit should always be effective, Mrs. Linde, but that's what I can't get Nora to grasp." Little does he know that his wife will make one of the most effective exits in the history of world theater.

Now, tipsy and alone with his wife, Torvald talks about his sexual fantasies. We discover that in his fantasies, as in real life, Torvald needs to dominate. Since he wants to make love to Nora, it's understandable that he's irritated when Rank enters.

Nora has changed since her last conversation with Rank. Since they are both thinking of an approaching death, Nora and Rank have become closer. Their conversation has special meaning that Torvald can't appreciate. Nora links herself with Rank by asking, "Tell me, what should we two go as at the next masquerade?" She knows perfectly well that masquerades are over for both of them.

As Rank leaves, Ibsen links them again. "Sleep well, Doctor," Nora says. "Thanks for that wish," Rank responds. "Wish me the same," she asks. "You? All right, if you like—Sleep well. And thanks for the light."

NOTE: You can read several meanings into Rank's last statement. Literally, he's thanking her for lighting his cigar. In the terminology of psychoanalytic theory, this reference has sexual overtones. Also, figuratively, Nora has been a light in his life.

Rank leaves and Torvald finally goes to check the mail. First he finds Rank's calling card marked with a black cross. Nora explains its meaning—Rank has gone home to die a solitary death. When Torvald remarks that they are now "thrown back upon each other, completely," you know that this is true. Nothing stands between husband and wife but the truth.

Torvald's next statement inadvertently assures Nora that her fantasy timetable is on schedule. "You know what, Nora?" he asks. "Time and again I've wished you were in some terrible danger, just so I could stake my life and soul and everything, for your sake."

Nora believes that her "miracle" is at hand. "Now you must read your mail, Torvald," she insists. She is about to leave to drown herself, when Torvald comes bursting out of his study to confront her.

When Nora admits that the charges in Krogstad's letter are true, Torvald is horrified. He immediately blames her, but still she clings to her hope. When she tells him she did it for love, he accuses her of "slippery tricks."

He has not yet performed "the miracle," so she prompts him. She won't let him suffer for her sake, she says. She won't let him take on her guilt.

But Torvald doesn't rise to the occasion. "Stop playacting!" he commands. In fact, Nora's whole idea of "the miracle" *was* only a fantasy. As her husband locks the hall door and begins to grill her, her illusions crumble. For the first time, she sees him as he really is. She's "beginning to understand everything now."

NOTE: As in the relationship between Kristine and Krogstad, the present has the power to change the past. Nora's sudden knowledge about her relationship to Torvald changes the meaning of eight years of marriage. This process cannot be reversed, even though Torvald will try to return things to the way they were.

Torvald responds in the same old ways. He is most concerned with appearances. He insists that he and Nora must act happily married—even though he won't sleep with her or let her near the children. He is even willing to pay off the blackmailer to save his reputation.

No sooner has Torvald shown his cowardice and disloyalty than another letter arrives. It contains

Nora's forged note and an apology from Krogstad. "I'm saved!" Torvald exults. "Nora, I'm saved!" Nora responds sardonically, "And I?" "You too, of course" is his reply.

Amazingly, but true to character, Torvald immediately tries to recreate the exact relationship he's just proved to be false. He goes even further. He explicitly invites Nora to rejoin him, not merely as a repentant wife, but as "his child as well." The doll should come back to her doll's house. Now you and Nora and even Torvald see the eight years of marriage in exactly the same light.

While Torvald talks, Nora goes into the bedroom to change. But instead of putting on her nightgown, she dresses in street clothes.

NOTE: Notice how often clothing is used symbolically throughout the play. This is especially true for Nora. She goes from wearing a brightly colored shawl when practicing the tarantella to wearing a black shawl to the party—the night she plans to die.

Nora sits Torvald down and begins their first serious talk—in the language of Torvald's world, a "settling of accounts."

NOTE: In the popular theater of the late nineteenth century, this play might have been put on in exactly the same way until this point. But in that theatrical tradition, there then would have been tears, pouts, and eventual reconciliation in a "happy ending." Ibsen departed from this tradition because he was concerned with the deeper issues of social and psychological truth. This direct and realistic talk between husband and wife has been called a breakthrough in modern drama. Why was such a conversation threatening to Ibsen's early audiences? Does it have the same effect today?

Nora explains to him what she's just discovered: she's never had a "self." She was a doll for her father, an echo of his opinions. Her marriage was merely a transfer from her father's house to Torvald's. Now she sees that during her eight years of marriage, she hasn't been a wife at all, but a pet, a performer who played a part to earn room and board.

Even more appalling to Nora is that she in turn is repeating the same pattern with the children. She has been teaching them to be subservient dolls in the same doll house.

Torvald claims to understand, but he doesn't have the slightest idea what she's talking about. He again lumps her with the children, promising to teach all of them how to behave better. Nora responds, "Oh, Torvald, you're not the man to teach me to be a good wife to you!"

She knows she is not yet capable of handling the job of raising children—there's another job she has to do first. She has to educate herself. To do that, she has to "stand completely alone, if I'm ever going to discover myself and the world out there."

NOTE: This statement of Nora's is one of the credos that Ibsen lived by. He repeated it often in letters and other writings. When, after this play opened, a female acquaintance turned up on his doorstep with her children in tow, saying, "I did it, I left him, just like Nora did," Ibsen replied, "Madam, Nora left *alone*."

Nora has her immediate future mapped out. She will go to stay with Kristine for the night, and then she will return to her hometown. A modern audience needs to keep in mind the seriousness of the step Nora is taking. The moment she walks out the door, she will be a social outcast—a woman who has deserted her husband and children. She will be seen as a moral cripple, much as Krogstad has been.

Torvald is quick to bring up this point. Her most sacred duties are to her family, he insists. Before all else she is a wife and mother. Here Torvald expresses the opinion of many members of Ibsen's audience. But Nora disagrees: "I believe that, before all else, I'm a human being, no less than you— or anyway, I ought to try to become one." As if defending her against the audience, Ibsen has her add, "I know the majority thinks you're right, Torvald, and plenty of books agree with you, too. But I . . . have to think over these things myself."

NOTE: This brings up another of Ibsen's favorite themes: the individual versus society. To him, society should serve the individual, but all too often it turns out the other way. Do you think Ibsen would still feel this is a pertinent issue in today's world? Why?

When Nora again says that she can't believe society's laws don't make allowances for a person acting out of love, Torvald insists, "You don't know anything of the world you live in." Nora intends to find out and to "discover who's right, the world or I." By asserting her right to know, she makes a claim on selfhood. She will not be just a daughter, a wife, a mother, but a person. This duty to oneself was important to Ibsen. Some may see this as pure selfishness. What is your reaction to a woman who leaves her husband and her children to find herself?

As Nora leaves her doll house, the final stage direction indicates that you hear the front door slamming shut. According to one commentator, it was "the door slam that was heard around the world."

NOTE: Will Nora Return?   Although these characters are fictional, ever since the play first appeared, readers and audiences everywhere have asked, will Nora return?

Ibsen's real-life model for Nora, Laura Kieler, eventually did return to her husband. At first, when Ibsen himself was asked the question, he said that Nora did return. But later, tired of the public outcry, he remarked, "How do I know? It is possible that she returns to husband and children, but also possible that she becomes an artiste in a travelling circus." The public reaction was so strongly opposed to Nora's act on moral grounds that it was performed with a variety of tacked-on happy endings in which Nora usually stays on and begs for forgiveness. Finally, to stop these total distortions Ibsen himself wrote an alternate ending in which

Nora collapses and stays because she can't leave her children. How would you react to this ending? What themes would you list for such a version?

The appropriate place to look for clues to Nora's future is in the play itself. When Torvald himself asks her if she'll return, she replies that it would take the "greatest miracle" to make it a "true marriage." Using only the play as evidence, try to answer the question yourself. How would you defend both sides? Consider the following questions as you gather evidence. Can Torvald transform himself? Could Nora love him again even if he changed? Would Nora's love for her children override other factors? Would Torvald take her back?

A STEP BEYOND

Test and Answers

TEST

1. Nora's macaroons symbolize _____
   A. Christmas
   B. a secret defiance of Torvald
   C. her flirtation with Dr. Rank

2. In the play we find that Nora _____
   I. doesn't understand the male worlds
      of money and business
   II. has had more to do with finance than
      Torvald knows
   III. has been able to save a nice nest egg
      for her family
   A. II and III only   B. I and II only
   C. I, II, and III

3. Ibsen gives us insight into Torvald's char- _____
   acter through his
   I. delight in travel
   II. attitude toward money
   III. use of pet names
   A. II only   B. I and II only
   C. II and III only

4. One of the play's major themes is _____
   A. women are stronger than men
   B. marriage is basically destructive
   C. "to thine own self be true"

5. Inherited "moral sickness" is attributed to _____

    A. Nora and Krogstad   B. Torvald
    C. venereal disease

6. Nora's "greatest miracle" will be that   _____
    A. she can find herself
    B. Rank won't die
    C. Torvald takes the blame for her
       forgery

7. Nora confides her biggest secret to Kristine   _____
  because
    A. Kristine told Nora her secrets
    B. Kristine thinks Nora is naive
    C. Nora needs help

8. According to *A Doll's House*,   _____
    A. men and women think alike
    B. men and women think differently, but
       both viewpoints are valid
    C. women need to learn how to survive
       in the business world

9. Nora feels she must die   _____
    A. to make clear her own responsibility
       for the forgery
    B. because she'll never be free of Torvald
    C. in order to serve as an object lesson
       for Torvald

10. Nora prepares for death by   _____
    I. dancing a wild dance
    II. writing a farewell letter to Torvald
  III. having a banquet
    A. I only   B. I and III only
    C. I, II, and III

11. Compare and contrast the rise and fall of the two
    couples: Nora and Torvald; Kristine and Krogstad.

12. What illusions shape Nora and Torvald's lives, and what forces Nora to confront reality?

13. In what ways are each of the other characters' situations similar to and different from Nora's?

14. Discuss the role of heredity and hereditary disease in *A Doll's House*.

15. Why does Nora have to leave at the end of the play? Will she ever return? Defend your position with evidence from the play.

ANSWERS

1. B **2.** B **3.** C **4.** C **5.** A **6.** C
7. B **8.** B **9.** A **10.** B

11. You might start by showing how things appear at the beginning. Nora and Torvald seem to have a happy marriage and a secure social position. Both Kristine and Krogstad appear to be lonely outcasts who have little to live for.

Then describe how these appearances start to crumble. Nora's marriage is based on deceptions and manipulation. Kristine, on the other hand, recognizes her own empty marriage and has accepted responsibility for her life. Kristine sees life realistically, while Nora hides from reality. Torvald and Krogstad both seek respectability, but Torvald is a pillar of society, while Krogstad is a forger.

Some of the circumstances that these couples have in common come to the surface. Nora is found to be guilty of the same crime that Krogstad once committed. She is in danger of morally infecting her children the same way that society feels Krogstad is ruining his.

Kristine and Krogstad are eventually able to look at the truth about themselves and each other. They can forgive each other and go about building a new life together. Nora and Torvald are also forced to see the truth about each other. However, while Nora realizes that their relationship and her life have been based on lies, Torvald refuses to admit they are lies. He can't forgive because, unlike Kristine and Krogstad, he still holds society's false values uppermost. While the truth saves Krogstad and Kristine, lies ruin Nora and Torvald.

12. Cite examples to show that Torvald thinks his wife is a doll, a toy, and a temptress with no ideas of her own. He thinks his house is free from debt; he believes he can control his family and his business decisions. He sees Rank only as his friend and ignores the doctor's relationship to Nora.

Nora at the outset believes that her husband is a good man who looks out for her best interests. She thinks she is an adult, a good wife and mother. She also thinks that secrets and manipulations are the normal ways to get what she wants. She treats life as a game that she knows how to play. She thinks that Torvald will be honorable and save her.

But Nora finds increasingly that reality intrudes. Dr. Rank is near death. The hidden loan is coming to the surface. She realizes that forgery even for love is a criminal act.

Krogstad's threat to reveal Nora's past act initiates the series of crises that forces Nora into reality. She is prepared for this by Rank's confession of his love. His imminent death will leave Nora and Torvald alone together. When the final crisis comes and they face each other, Nora's last illusion is shattered. She finds out that Torvald is looking out for himself, not her. In fact, no one is looking out for her. This is a role she must take on herself. She must leave her "doll's house" to become a person.

13. There are many parallel situations in the play. They call attention to the different ways each situation might be worked out. You might cite specific examples—for example, Torvald and Nora mirror each other at the beginning of the play because they both favor appearance over reality. This calls attention to the contrast between them at the end when she has the strength to reject appearances.

Kristine's former marriage parallels Nora's. It was an empty sham. Kristine married to get money for a good cause the same way that Nora illegally borrowed money for a good cause. However, in contrast to Nora, Kristine knows what she has done and is ready for a new life.

Krogstad and Nora are in similar situations. They are both accused of passing on moral sickness to their children. They are also both considered to have contracted their sickness from a parent. Krogstad, however, is an outcast, while she is respected. He knows he has committed a crime, while Nora sees her act as a gesture of love.

Dr. Rank, Krogstad, and Nora all have an "inherited" sickness that must be faced. Nora and Dr. Rank play at love (like Nora and Torvald). They both face death, and at the end of the play, both are in a sense released to "a greater beyond." Unlike that of Nora or Krogstad, Rank's sickness is not purely moral so he is condemned to certain death. Nora's death, however, is a self-created fantasy based on wishful thinking. Also, unlike Rank, Nora refuses to acknowledge her feelings for him as well as his for her.

Anne-Marie, the nursemaid, parallels Nora because she gave up her child to be raised by someone else. In contrast to Nora, she had to do it for social and economic reasons. Nora proposes to give up her children for moral reasons.

There are other examples of parallelism and contrast that you might choose instead.

14. Heredity is first introduced when it is disclosed that Dr. Rank is dying of an unnamed disease he was born with, and for which his father's immoral ways were in some sense responsible. The term *heredity* as used in the play could also be considered as environmental influence or psychological conditioning. Torvald insists that someone like Krogstad is a criminal because he had a dishonest mother. This implies that Nora's children are in moral danger of "catching" dishonesty from her. Torvald also assures Nora that she inherited her ineptitude with money from her father. The connection between the moral condition of a parent and child is reinforced by Dr. Rank's references to children suffering for the sins of their fathers (or other family members) in Act 2.

Other forces of so-called heredity or parental transmission are at work. Nora learned compliance from her father and has transferred this relationship to Torvald. She is teaching her children to be unthinking and compliant the same way she was taught. To her, this is more dangerous than passing on dishonesty. However, we see the possibility of thwarting "heredity," or past conditioning, in Krogstad's conversion by love and Nora's by intellectual self-realization.

15. It seems that Nora has to leave because the situation in her home will not allow her to discover who she is and how to live truthfully. She and Torvald have never had a serious discussion, and Torvald shows no signs of knowing how to start. His deeply ingrained gender role is dependent on her being passive and innocent (ignorant?). Moreover, he considers her deeply guilty of moral corruption and a danger to his children. He lacks compassion. When the crisis passes, he insists on treating her like a child again.

Nora, on the other hand, has to take time to question the attitudes she's been spoon-fed. Is society right? Is the church right? Is Torvald right? Maybe there's truth on all sides, but she's never thought it out for herself. She feels she must remove herself from this false relationship before she can begin to discover if it can become constructive.

Will Nora ever return? If you choose to argue that she will, find evidence to support the view that (a) Torvald will change; (b) Nora will find a way to compromise; (c) Nora will not be able to cope on her own without her children; (d) Nora will realize her "folly"; or a similar argument.

If you choose to say she will never return, argue that (a) Torvald will never change; (b) Nora couldn't accept any marriage situation of that era; (c) she couldn't forgive Torvald for his rejection; (d) she never really loved Torvald; (e) she can make it on her own in the world; or another similar position.

Remember to support your view with evidence of Nora's and Torvald's characters drawn from the play.

Term Paper Ideas and other Topics for Writing

The Play and Literary Topics

1. *A Doll's House* as a breakthrough in modern theater.

2. Ibsen's use of visual symbols in *A Doll's House*, including set, props, and costumes.

3. Ibsen's use of dramatic irony in *A Doll's House*.

4. The significance of past action in *A Doll's House*.

5. Nora and Torvald's fantasies; how they shape the play.

6. Ibsen as a humanist, or Ibsen's road to *A Doll's House*.

7. How *A Doll's House* evolved into *Ghosts*.

8. Psychology and the subconscious in *A Doll's House*.

9. An analysis of alternate endings produced for *A Doll's House*.

Themes

1. Women in a masculine world: *A Doll's House* and *Hedda Gabler*.

2. Nora's search for self.

3. Truth as constructive and destructive in *A Doll's House*.

4. Nora and Torvald as symbols of male and female.

5. Heredity and disease in *A Doll's House*.

6. The theme of death in *A Doll's House*.

7. How the present is "pregnant with the past" in *A Doll's House*.

8. Society and the individual in *A Doll's House*.

9. Appearance and reality in *A Doll's House*.

10. Reactions to *A Doll's House*: in Ibsen's time and today.

Structure

1. The *pièce bien faite*: how Ibsen transcended it.

2. The "unrelenting cohesion" (unity) of *A Doll's House*.

3. The role of fate and past actions in *Oedipus Rex* and *A Doll's House*.

Hedda Gabler

THE PLAY

The Plot

On a lovely September morning, Miss Juliana Tesman comes to call on her nephew George and his new wife, Hedda. They've just returned from a six-month wedding trip, during which George has also done research on a book. George recently received a doctorate and will soon be appointed a professor. It's obvious that George loves his aunt Juliana and just as obvious that Hedda despises both of them. George, however, appears oblivious to Hedda's feelings.

Hedda's old schoolmate, Thea Elvsted, comes to call. In school Thea used to be terrified of Hedda, who pulled her blonde hair and threatened to burn it off. Thea and George were once interested in each other. Now Hedda appears sweet and understanding as Thea tells her story.

She is involved in a loveless marriage and has fallen in love with Eilert Løvborg, her stepchildren's tutor. Løvborg was once George's main rival for the professorship, but had become an alcoholic and a man given to excess. However, with Thea's help he has reformed and written a very successful book. He has come back to town, and Thea has left her husband to follow him—largely because she loves him, but partly because she's afraid he'll slide back into his old habits. Thea is not completely sure of Løvborg's feelings for her. He still thinks about an old lover who once threatened to shoot him with a pistol.

Judge Brack, a friend of the family, announces that Løvborg once again is George's rival and a strong contender for the academic post. George is frantic because he's bought a huge, expensive house on his future prospects. Hedda, although disappointed that she might lose luxuries, is looking forward to the contest between the two.

The next day, while George is away visiting his Aunt Juliana and her fatally ill sister Rina, Judge Brack returns to visit Hedda. Brack used to be one of Hedda's suitors and now wants to have a secret affair with her. Although the two are friends and speak freely with each other, Hedda is not interested in a closer relationship. She admits her coolness to him, her terrible boredom with life, and her need to make others suffer.

Løvborg comes to call on Tesman. He has written a second book, this one even more brilliant. When he and Hedda are left alone, they reveal their past secret romance. She is the former lover that Thea spoke of, who had threatened to shoot him. Hedda had been thrilled by Løvborg's thirst for life, but when he became serious about her, she rejected him and made her dramatic threat.

Hedda tells Løvborg that Thea doesn't trust him. In Thea's presence, Hedda goads him into having a drink and going with George and Brack to a party later that night. Thea will wait with Hedda til he returns. Although Thea is desperately worried about him, Hedda is sure that Løvborg will become "free" and return with vine leaves in his hair, her symbol for someone who defies society.

Neither of the men returns that night. George is the first one back in the morning, and he has the manuscript of Løvborg's second book, his masterpiece, with him. Løvborg was so drunk that he carelessly dropped the manuscript. When George reads a note that his Aunt Rina is dying, he rushes qrout, leaving the manuscript with Hedda.

Brack arrives to tell Hedda that after Løvborg left the judge's, he went on to a party at Mademoiselle Diana's, a redheaded "singer." When Løvborg realized his manuscript was missing, he started a fight at her place, hit a policeman, and was arrested. Brack warns Hedda not to take Løvborg in.

Then Løvborg returns to the Gabler house and tells Thea he has no more use for her and has torn up the manuscript. Furious because it was their "child" he has destroyed, she leaves.

Instead of telling Løvborg she has the manuscript, Hedda agrees that his life is hopeless and encourages him to end it "beautifully" by his own hand with one of her father's pistols. After he leaves with the gun, she pulls out the manuscript and burns it in the stove, admitting that she's killing Thea and Løvborg's "child."

When George returns and asks for the manuscript, Hedda says she burned it for his sake. (Its brilliance would have guaranteed Løvborg the professorship.) She also hints that she's pregnant. George is overwhelmed by these evidences of her "love." They are joined by Thea, who is again worried about Løvborg. Brack brings the news that Løvborg has shot himself and is dying. Everyone else is appalled—but Hedda is ecstatic.

George feels deeply guilty over Løvborg's death and the destruction of his manuscript. But Thea has the original notes for the book. She and George agree to rewrite it. Thea will become the same "inspiration" to George that she was to his rival.

Quietly, Judge Brack tells Hedda the truth about Løvborg. He was killed, not by a suicidal act, but accidentally when his gun discharged while he was at Mademoiselle Diana's. A deliberate bullet through the temple (an acceptable tradition in affairs of honor) would have been a "beautiful" act to Hedda, but the accidental wound to the stomach merely disgusts her. This is the final evidence that she has no power over anyone; there is no longer hope for beauty, as she knows it, in the world.

George talks Thea into moving to his Aunt Juliana's so they can work together every night. In a blackmail attempt, Brack tells Hedda that he knows Løvborg was killed with her gun and that he'll divulge this information unless she becomes his mistress. Feeling trapped and powerless, Hedda goes into the back room, plays a wild dance on her piano, and then shoots herself "beautifully" in the temple.

The Characters*

Hedda Gabler

What is it that makes Hedda Gabler Tesman so fascinating that Ibsen wrote a whole play to explore her character? Do you know someone like her who is dangerous to be involved with, but interesting to watch? What fascinates us about de-

*Spelling of the characters' names may vary according to the translation.

structive and manipulative characters in movies and television shows?

In *Hedda Gabler*, Ibsen portrays a disturbed yet fascinating woman. Hedda is complex, not easy to understand; she has so many "faces." Here are some clues to her personality:

1.   Hedda is predatory and selfish. She sees others merely as a way to get what she wants. If someone like Thea has something good like Løvborg, Hedda wants it for herself. If she can't have it, she wants to destroy it.

2.   Hedda is empty. She has no life of her own so she chooses to live others' lives either through vicarious substitution or by exercising power over them. With Løvborg she does both: in the past she vicariously lived his wild sprees and now she wants to control the kind of life (and death) he chooses.

3.   Hedda has little emotional capacity. She has spent so many years trying to conform to her father's wishes and to society's conventions that she has no idea who she is or how she really feels about things. Because of this, she is incapable of loving or being intimate with or even considerate of others. When Løvborg became too serious, she threatened to shoot him. Comradeship describes her past relationship with Løvborg and her easy way with Judge Brack.

4.   Hedda is dominated by the past. Some suggest that General Gabler dominates Hedda's psyche the way his portrait dominates Ibsen's set for the play. You can guess from her upbringing that her father wanted a boy. She has the military's respect for rank and power, which she uses to push around the weak, like Aunt Julie and Thea. The female

side of her nature seems to have been sublimated, with serious psychological consequences. Being a woman seems worthless, so she hates other women and tries to make them feel worthless too.

5.   Hedda is trapped by society. She'd like to live a daring, creative life but is afraid of society's condemnation. Her fear of scandal may be due to her father's military background, with its emphasis on discipline and conformity to rules.

6.   Hedda is a coward. She's afraid of acting out her inner desires because she has no confidence in herself.

7.   Hedda is attracted to death. Her favorite toys are her father's pistols, obvious symbols of death. She calls suicide "a free and courageous action . . . that shimmers with spontaneous beauty." Lending Løvborg one of the pistols so that he can end his life "beautifully" gives her a feeling of power. Hedda's own death at the end may be her ultimate mode of self-expression. Her attraction to an honorable death and to suicide may have come from the combination of military tradition with popular nineteenth-century Romantic ideas about love and death. These ideas glorified suicide as a response to failed ambitions.

8.   Hedda is, most of all, a bundle of contradictions. Her superior intelligence is at war with inner forces that not even Hedda can understand. She seems both predator and prey. She feels intensely but cannot express anything except negative words and actions. She loves freedom but is afraid to act. She is female, yet hates femininity. She wants to be with men but threatens to shoot them if they

want too much from her. She hates weak people and is herself a coward.

One might sum up Hedda's contradictions in the fact that she often detests something (for example, life, society, or men) at the same time she desires it. She starts an action, then sabotages it. Her "thirst for life" becomes perverted into death. Her only courageous action (suicide) is the end of all action.

Some readers feel that the play is weakened because Hedda doesn't change and evolve. She seems the same bundle of neuroses at the end of the play that she is at the beginning. Others feel that the point of the play isn't to change Hedda, but to watch fate bring about the logical conclusion to her personality and actions.

What do you think? What makes Hedda the way she is? Is there any way she could have been saved?

George Tesman

George Tesman is a man devoted to scholarship and to study of the past. While his wife seems an emotional slave to the past, George is its intellectual servant. He appears neither to see nor to care much about what is going on around him.

Steady and devoted to giving his wife the material pleasures she demands, he asks no emotional involvement and accepts Hedda on her own terms. George collects things, and a wife like Hedda is simply another prize in his collection.

He is a "specialist"—his interests are as narrow as is his way of thinking. Tesman's research on "domestic handicrafts in medieval Brabant" shows he is most at home amid the trivia of cultures long ago and far away. He is also good at collecting and filing other people's data. In short, he is not a creative thinker. He is in his glory when preserving, restoring, and reconstructing what is dead; he interacts more easily with Løvborg's ideas after Løvborg is dead and his ideas have become history.

He accepts society and plays by its rules. So far, he has been rewarded by a good marriage (in his eyes) and the promise of a professorship.

Is George a credible character? Or has Ibsen exaggerated his faults and made him an easy target for Hedda's contempt?

Whether you feel that George represents the society that stifles Hedda and pushes her boredom to its limit or see him as a harmless, decent academic who tries to do his best, he certainly becomes Hedda's victim in a marriage of convenience that backfires.

Aunt Juliana Tesman

Aunt Juliana seems kind and lovable but her role has generated controversy. In the eyes of some, she has accepted her femininity and finds true happiness by serving others. She raised George after his parents died and has been caring for her invalid sister for many years. She keeps trying to welcome Hedda to the family despite the many obvious insults that come from her new niece-in-law. She is thrilled for George that Hedda is pregnant. When her sister Rina dies, she mourns, then selflessly vows to take care of someone else.

On the other hand, some readers question this "selfless" love as a dishonest cover for selfish motives. They see Aunt Julie's role as a stinging attack on this kind of smothering love. She only seems to love people who are helpless and dependent.

When Rina dies, she won't take in just any boarder; she'll look for another invalid. By the same token, some feel that she's purposely kept George from maturing and taking responsibility for himself. She keeps others dependent to fill a void in herself. Of course she's thrilled that Hedda is pregnant—that will mean one more helpless human being in the world.

Although Hedda and Aunt Julie seem worlds apart, they share an inability to live for themselves. Some might even say that Aunt Julie has destroyed George (as a man) as effectively as Hedda destroys Løvborg.

Thea Elvsted

Thea's role as Løvborg's inspiration and Hedda's friend obviously sets her up for comparison with Hedda. How are they alike and how do they differ?

Unlike Hedda, Thea is in touch with her femininity. This allows her to be loving and supportive. She can give herself completely to Løvborg. Also unlike Hedda, Thea has the courage to defy society and leave her loveless marriage when it gets in the way of her true self.

However, some might say that Thea wants to live through Løvborg (and later George) as much as Hedda does. Her inspirational role is nothing but an attempt to find the self-affirmation she doesn't get in her own marriage. Is Thea devoted to Løvborg or to being needed and involved? After all, when he dies she hardly mourns but goes on with George to recreate these ideas.

You might also compare her with Aunt Julie. Is Thea selfless or selfish? Has she found a true self-expressing femininity or does she use her nurturing tendencies to mold others into the kind of people she needs them to be?

Judge Brack

Brack, a friend of the Gablers, is linked to Hedda's father in one obvious way—they are both referred to by titles instead of first names. One is a judge, the other a general: they both represent established institutions of society.

Brack is drawn to Hedda. They both have contempt for the rules. At the same time, they both fear scandal and a loss of respectability. They are equals who enjoy each other's company and can speak freely with one another. But Hedda wants them equal as men and won't accept his sexual overtures. Hedda threatens to shoot him as she had threatened Løvborg when he tried to get close.

Brack is as selfish as Hedda. He also wants power over others. But unlike Hedda in that nineteenth-century European society, he is a man and can have a profession, causes, and goals outside the home. If he is emotionally empty, he does not have to commit himself to the intimacy of marriage. Brack can remain respectable while pursuing affairs with married women like Hedda. Ibsen is showing a clear example of the double standard at work.

Brack has greater access to power and fulfillment than Hedda has, but is even more ruthless. Blackmail doesn't faze him at all. He cares nothing for others' feelings. He is the perfect character to have ultimate power over Hedda: she is terrified of scandal and public opinion; and he wouldn't hesitate to involve her in the shooting of Løvborg or in an adulterous situation with himself. His blackmail threat is the immediate cause of Hedda's final suicidal act of "liberation."

Eilert Løvborg

Perhaps the most sympathetic character in the play, Løvborg has a flamboyant and creative brilliance. He has a true thirst for life and is the only one who can evoke that passion in Hedda. By the same token, he is the only one who recognizes her cowardly retreat behind conventions, and he confronts her with it.

He rejects compromise and seeks self-awareness. His thoughts and actions must be in harmony, even if that means turning his back on society, as he does. Once free, Eilert is able to write the books that express his creativity.

To Ibsen, the person in that society who rejects compromise must meet with catastrophe. And Løvborg does, partly through the manipulations of Hedda, who thrusts him back into the old ways he abhors, and partly through his own weakness. He has a fatal flaw: he is an alcoholic who equates freedom with debauchery.

Some readers who admire Løvborg feel that Ibsen had to use him sparingly to maintain the course of the play. First, Løvborg is so strong and passionate that he could move Hedda toward feelings that might change her. Second, he is so sympathetic and engaging that he could cause you to care about him, so you would be pulling for him, instead of objectively watching the part he plays.

Other readers feel that Løvborg is erratic at best. Ibsen has put him in a double bind. Løvborg can only be "free" when defying society, but he can only be productive when he's controlling his destructive impulses. He cannot be free and productive at the same time.

Some feel that the most damning criticism of Løvborg is that his "freedom" isn't any different from Brack's. There is nothing significant or revolutionary in Løvborg's defiance: he just isn't able to control his excesses.

Is Løvborg a genius who knows himself and is truly free? Or is he a slave to his excesses?

Other Elements
SETTING

Hedda Gabler takes place in an unnamed Norwegian city. The setting is a large rambling house that once belonged to a cabinet minister. This mansion may represent the declining aristocracy, to whose ideals and trapping Hedda is still loyal. The house is much too large and much too expensive for the Tesmans. What's more, it has an "odor of death."

As in *A Doll's House* and some of his other works, Ibsen's descriptions of the setting are lengthy and detailed, and reveal much about the major characters, particularly Hedda Gabler. We are in a large drawing room "decorated in dark colors." Outside, the trees are "in autumn colors." Hedda is also dark and melancholy and, at twenty-nine, seems already to be passing through the autumn of her life.

Behind the drawing room is a darker inner room, which suggests Hedda's innermost thoughts, or in psychological terminology, her subconscious. This small room is dominated by a portrait of the late General Gabler, who still dominates Hedda. During the play, we see Hedda retreat more and more into herself until she finally enters this "inner room" to die in the company of the dead general.

THEMES

As the title suggests, *Hedda Gabler* is more a character study than a play about social problems. However, some of the themes of Ibsen's "problem" plays recur. Here are major themes of the play.

1. SOCIETY AND THE INDIVIDUAL

As in *A Doll's House*, this play describes a society that "sacrifices to itself freedom and individual expression." It opposes the true self-expression of Hedda (as a woman) and Løvborg (as a creative spirit). It approves of Aunt Juliana's mothering self-sacrifice and George's mediocrity, and elevates to positions of authority men like Judge Brack, a manipulator who cares little for the law and less for people.

This theme is emphasized in the comparison between Thea and Hedda. While Thea (whose husband is an official of society) flouts the rules to be with Løvborg, Hedda fears scandal and lacks the courage to act on her beliefs. How much of Hedda's fate is caused by society rather than her personality is open to interpretation.

2. CONFLICT BETWEEN IDEALS AND ACTION

Have you ever known what you *should* do in a situation, but didn't do it? Did this make you feel torn inside? Ibsen knew that this was a common human problem. In this play, Thea has the strength to turn her thoughts into action by leaving her husband, whom she knows she doesn't love. Hedda, on the other hand, has Løvborg's individualistic convictions and visions of life, but conforms to George's life-style. She senses the gap but cannot bridge it. Løvborg's ideals are not realized either because of his inner weakness. This inner conflict drives both Hedda and Løvborg to despair and, possibly, to their deaths.

3. THE STRUGGLE FOR SELF-REALIZATION

To Ibsen, self-knowledge was very important. You shouldn't be forced into a mold by society or family, nor should you drift aimlessly through life. Identifying your own uniqueness and special needs is a preliminary to a productive life. Although Hedda is aware of her inner conflicts, it can be argued that she never finds a true self. Perhaps she finds two selves that cannot be reconciled. Although Løvborg makes headway in his search, he, too, cannot resolve his vision with his weakness.

Thea Elvsted seems to come closest to realizing her true nature and her relationship with society. She leaves her family for love but doesn't reject society's constraints altogether. She helps Løvborg to control his excesses (antisocial tendencies) so that he can be productive. Their manuscript could be interpreted as a true product of self-awareness, love, and ideals.

4. CHRISTIAN VERSUS PAGAN BEHAVIOR

Ibsen wasn't happy with the Christian idea of selfless giving. He felt that extreme selflessness was really just a form of selfishness. For example, Aunt Juliana nurses invalids not for their own sake but to meet her own need to be depended on. Some might interpret Thea's support for Løvborg and her later collaboration with George as over-giving.

On the other hand, the pagan religion of the ancient Greeks and Romans incorporated what Ibsen considered to be healthy outlets for self-expression in ritualistic orgies. Both Hedda and Løvborg link wild "pagan" behavior with freedom. Of course, such behavior is also a prelude to death. Does *Hedda Gabler* say that there is an evitable connection between freedom and death? If so, how can this view be defended? Is restraint of excess being upheld or denounced?

5. WOMEN IN A MASCULINE WORLD

While Nora in *A Doll's House* seems to be a woman caught in an oppressive masculine society, Hedda seems to be caught in a male image she has of herself. Her oppression arises because she cannot be a man and share in men's society. Men are allowed to drink, carouse, and express themselves frankly while women must be discreet and restrained. As you read, ask yourself whether Hedda is the product of a male-oriented society or the prisoner of a peculiar attachment to her father, or both.

STYLE

One of the chief hallmarks of Ibsen's style during his Realistic Period (1877–1890) is its everyday, conversational quality. Like *A Doll's House*, *Hedda Gabler* contains only short, prose dialogue. There are no poetic interludes or long speeches. Even though intellectual ideas play an important part in *Hedda Gabler*, they are not discussed at length. For example, the contents of Tesman's research and Løvborg's two books are only briefly mentioned.

Before Ibsen, ordinary language was not used in serious drama. It was limited to light comedies and romances like the popular French *pièces biens faites* (see pages 24-25). Ibsen decided to use the language (and theatrical devices) of these "well-made plays" in his works about conventional, middle-class people. One of the problems a translator faces in converting Ibsen's works from Norwegian to English is how to capture the impression of ordinariness that struck his audiences. There are two major obstacles: first, the Norwegian of Ibsen's era was fundamentally more formal than English and, second, the "everyday" speech of the educated middle class then was more formal than middle-class speech is today.

The following translation of *Hedda Gabler* was used in the preparation of this guide: Henrik Ibsen, *Four Major Plays*, Vol. I, translated by Rolf Fjelde, Signet Classic, 1965.

To keep the tone of his plays conversational, Ibsen used brief, significant phrases to convey to the audience a total picture or more than one meaning. For example, Hedda's vision of Løvborg with "vine leaves in his hair," would bring to mind Dionysus (Bacchus), the mythological Greek god of wine and his drunken orgies.

More often, single words carry the weight. For example, George's use of Thea Elvsted's maiden name, Rysing, indicates a premarital romantic interest. "Comrades" ("companions") is a code word for Hedda's idea of the ultimate relationship with a man. Judge Brack's reference to the cold punch as "poison" alerts you to its real effect on Løvborg, a reformed alcoholic.

Because Ibsen was so interested in economy of

style, he frequently placed the burden of meaning on visual objects rather than words. You have only to think of Hedda's pistols and piano, George's slippers, Aunt Julie's hat, and General Gabler's portrait, to name a few. That is why it is so important to read the stage directions, which describe the set and the characters' appearances and clothes.

For additional discussion of Ibsen's style, turn to pages 22-24.

FORM AND STRUCTURE

In *Hedda Gabler*, Ibsen has again taken the basic form of the French *pièce bien faite* (see Form and Structure, pages 24-25). There are guilty secrets, past relationships, and a blackmail threat.

The play is tightly constructed. There are only six major characters and a single set. The time frame is about three days. All the characters have had previous relationships with each other; they are linked romantically and socially.

Let's look at the pattern of action in the four acts.

Act One: This act introduces the characters and Hedda's marital situation, and reveals past action.

Act Two: The action begins to build. The nature of Hedda's relationships with Løvborg and Brack is explored as she attempts to defeat Thea and control Løvborg's destiny.

Act Three: The play builds to a climax as Hedda sends Løvborg off to commit suicide and then burns his "lost" book.

Act Four: The action falls as everything unwinds. Hedda is defeated. Realizing that she is powerless, she commits suicide.

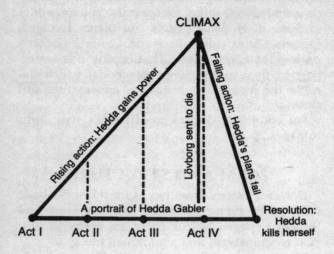

The Story
ACT ONE

There's excitement at the Tesman's new house—
George Tesman and his wife, Hedda, have returned from a six-month honeymoon. George's
aunt, Miss Juliana Tesman, is the first visitor. From
her discussion with Berta the maid, you discover
that Aunt Julie raised George after his parents'
death.

NOTE: Selflessness In this conversation you find
clues to Aunt Julie's personality. Earlier she cared
for George, and now she's caring for her sister
Rina, who has been an invalid for years. You can
see her concern for George's well-being as he em-

barks on married life. As you read, consider how Aunt Julie's care has affected George. Has she kept him from maturing? Does his independence please her? What do you think Ibsen is saying about her devotion? Is it as selfless as it seems?

Aunt Julie and Berta's talk also serves to reveal important background information to the audience. George has received his doctorate while on the trip and is now a contender for a position as professor. He has made a good match by marrying the daughter of General Gabler.

NOTE: The two women never call Hedda by name. She is either "the young bride" or "General Gabler's daughter." This and the huge picture of the general that hangs prominently in the inner room are our first clues to the general's influence over Hedda. The biggest clue, of course, lies in the title of the play. Ibsen is preparing you to meet Hedda Gabler, not Hedda Tesman. As you watch Hedda in action during the play, you should be able to answer the question: Why did Ibsen call this play *Hedda Gabler*?

When George enters, he fusses over his aunt, calls her by affectionate pet names, and notices especially the new hat she is wearing for Hedda's sake. Instead of discussing the honeymoon, he happily tells Aunt Julie about all the wonderful old manuscripts he got to read. He was able to afford this lengthy trip only by combining it with research.

Aunt Julie's news isn't so good. Aunt Rina is failing, and Julie worries that she'll have no one to live for if Rina should die.

They go on to discuss the house. It is a large, luxurious house, well out of George's price range. But Hedda had her heart set on it, so Judge Brack arranged easy terms, and Aunt Julie took out a mortgage on her pension. Again, she notes that it's her pleasure to help this poor, parentless boy.

We do see a bit of spite in Aunt Julie. She tells George she's glad that the ones who have tried to keep him from succeeding have fallen. And "the one most dangerous to you—he fell furthest." This is a foreshadowing of the rivalry between George and Eilert Løvborg (his old academic rival) over both academic advancement and Hedda that forms a central part of the play's action.

Løvborg is rumored to have written a new book. But, since Løvborg drinks heavily, George and Aunt Julie think the book can hardly amount to much. This prompts George to talk excitedly about *his* new book—on the "domestic handicrafts of Brabant in the Middle Ages." It may be hard for you to get excited over such a topic, but that's just the point Ibsen is making about Tesman.

NOTE: George's work is a good indication of George's personality. He is caught in the past, and his thinking is far from creative or original. He collects and analyzes the trivia of a distant time and place. He even considers Hedda a beautiful collector's item. The way the past affects different characters reveals a lot about them. Compare especially how Hedda and George are each so affected.

You've already had a number of hints about Hedda before she arrives. Is the detailed picture Ibsen now presents what you had envisioned? According to the author, Hedda is well-bred, distinguished, and stylish, with a pallid complexion and "steel gray eyes [that] express a cool, unruffled calm." What do you think Ibsen is telling you right away about this woman?

Aunt Julie's natural impulse is to be warm and kind, but Hedda has no intention of letting this new relative get close. With amazing speed, Hedda lampoons each act of kindness Aunt Julie performs. She refuses to call the aunt by her first name, implies that she has come too early, grumbles about all the flowers in the room, and shows no interest in George's old bedroom slippers that Aunt Julie has brought over. Most cruelly, Hedda refers to Aunt Julie's new bonnet as the maid's "old hat."

NOTE: Visual Information   Ibsen relies heavily on visual details to convey information about the characters. George's slippers are a concrete reminder of his childhood and childlike reliance on his aunt. Aunt Julie's hat is a visual reminder of Hedda's cruelty and the aunt's good intentions.

In the preliminary set descriptions for Act One, Ibsen has already called attention to General Gabler's portrait, the inner room, the piano, the dark colors, the season, and Hedda's hair color. These and other features will take on added meaning as the play progresses. Watch for the appearance of Hedda's most important possessions for a clue to her personality.

Aunt Julie only recovers from these slights when

George indicates that Hedda may be pregnant. Aunt
Julie is thrilled at the idea of a child to coddle. But
Hedda angrily denies her condition. The reason
for her anger will become evident as you get to
know Hedda better.

When George and Aunt Julie leave and Hedda
is alone, she *"moves about the room, raising her arms
and clenching her fists as if in a frenzy."* She says
nothing. What message do you get from these gestures to add to your picture of her?

NOTE: This is the first of several silent interludes
when Hedda is alone on stage. These moments
suggest that Hedda's motivations are hidden and
that she has difficulty in expressing her true self,
but that violent emotions lie deep.

George returns and Hedda remarks that her old
piano—like George's slippers, a symbol of the past—
doesn't fit the decor. Instead of trading it in, as
George suggests, she wants to move it into the
adjoining inner room and get a new one in its place.
Hedda obviously feels that her past and present
don't fit together. Remember that the small room
also houses her father's portrait.

Hedda finds flowers and a calling card from a
Mrs. Thea Elvsted, one of George's old flames and
a former schoolmate of Hedda's. No sooner has
she read the card than Berta comes in to announce
Thea's arrival.

NOTE: Hedda first identifies Thea as "the one
with the irritating hair that she was always show-

ing off." Ibsen goes out of his way to describe the hair of three female characters in this play. Hedda's is "an attractive medium brown, but not particularly abundant." Thea's, by contrast, is "almost a white-gold, and unusually abundant and wavy," suggesting femininity. Pay close attention to other references to Thea's hair—and to the third character whose hair will be described and commented upon shortly.

Thea is agitated about something. She has come from the country and knows no one in town except the Tesmans. Hedda encourages her to disclose what is bothering her. Thea tells her story, which becomes more and more interesting to Hedda.

Thea had married a much older widower with children, who hired Eilert Løvborg, George's old academic rival, as a tutor. While he lived with the Elvsteds out in the country, Thea helped him to stop drinking, which enabled him to write a brilliant book—the one that George has heard about. Now that the book is a success, Løvborg has left the Elvsteds and come back into town. Afraid he will return to his old ways, Thea asks George to keep an eye on him. Hedda seems interested but doesn't press the matter until George leaves to write a note of invitation to Eilert.

NOTE: Thea There are two ways to interpret Thea's fears about Løvborg's return to town; which way you choose will influence your interpretation of the play. Some readers feel that Thea selflessly helped Løvborg to find himself, that she represents womanhood at its best and is justifiably concerned when he returns to the temptations of city life. Others feel that she pushed him into the narrow mold of academic and social responsibility, stifling his true genius. Her search for him and her fears that he can't make it on his own suggest the somewhat suffocating love of Aunt Juliana for George. Is she supportive or stifling? Is she acting out of concern or to reassert her control? As the action unfolds you may be better able to assess Thea Elvsted.

Hedda moves in to get control of Thea. There is a challenge to this: Thea's instinct is not to trust Hedda. In school, she reminds Hedda, "whenever we met on the stairs, you'd always pull my hair . . . and once you said you would burn it off." Hedda worms out of Thea that her marriage is emotionally bankrupt and she's fallen in love with Løvborg. In fact, she's packed up and left her husband to be with him. Hedda's first reaction is to wonder "that you could dare to do such a thing! . . . But what do you think people will say about you, Thea?"

NOTE: This is the first hint of Hedda's serious concern with what other people think. Like Nora in *A Doll's House*, there is no fulfillment for her in society's setup. But unlike Nora, Hedda is immobilized by her fear of scandal. It matters a great deal to her what people think. Ibsen's notes on Hedda said, "There is profound poetry in Hedda, but her surroundings frighten her." Yet she is fascinated by other people's rebellion. She lives somewhat like a vampire, feeding on other people's courage and freedom.

Thea loves Løvborg enough not to care, but she reveals her uncertainty about whether he returns the feeling. She acknowledges that there is an unknown woman's shadow between them, someone who once threatened Løvborg with a pistol. Hedda responds coolly that "nobody behaves that way around here." Thea's suspicion innocently falls on "that redheaded singer" who's come back to town. Here is the third female character Ibsen identifies by her hair. You will learn more later about this woman.

The act now shifts attention from Thea to a new character, Judge Brack. A powerful and important man, he knows what's going on around town. He is also a respected authority figure like Hedda's late father. Like Hedda herself, he is distinguished. Unlike Hedda, he has eyes that are "bright and lively." The news he brings ties in with the news that Thea has already revealed. It seems that Løvborg's book is so remarkable that it's restored his reputation, and he is once again a competitor for the professorship that George expects will be his. George is devastated. He has married Hedda and bought the house on the assumption that he would soon have a professor's salary. He will be in deep financial trouble if he doesn't get the post.

Hedda, by contrast, is exhilarated. There is finally a worthy game being played in her parlor, "a championship match" between George and Løvborg. After reminding her that she will have no money or position if George loses the post, Brack leaves.

Hedda can't believe that George would really be left without money. From her point of view, their marriage was a business contract, and his part of the bargain was that she'd have a fancy house and a place in society. Society and its trappings matter to Hedda. Without money, she will have only one source of amusement left: General Gabler's pistols. She is as attached to these as George is to his old slippers.

Though we don't see the pistols, we note Tesman's horrified reaction when Hedda goes to get them. Ibsen has set up one of the theater's oldest devices: the loaded gun that must go off before the play ends.

ACT TWO

The opening scene of Act Two focuses on General Gabler's pistols. Hedda is alone, loading one of them. She threatens, in a seemingly serious tone, to shoot Judge Brack, who has come through the garden to call on George. Hedda fires the gun, shooting up into the air. Brack angrily chastises her as if she were a naughty child, takes the pistol, and puts it into its case. It is now pretty obvious that Hedda is the "shadow" between Thea and Løvborg.

NOTE: The general's pistols are Hedda's most powerful symbols. They are her link to her father. They also link her romantically with both Eilert Løvborg, whom she had formerly threatened to shoot, and Judge Brack, who says that he knows those pistols. The pistols seem to be Hedda's only means of defying society and expressing herself.

But why does Hedda express herself so nega-
tively? Why has she threatened both a lover and
a friend?

Hedda's relationship with Brack reveals more of
her than you've seen so far. She speaks openly
with him, as an equal. Brack thinks he knows how
Hedda's mind works. "Are you still playing
games?" Brack shows his past sexual interest in
Hedda hasn't changed even though she is now
married. The witty thrust and counterthrust of their
conversation demonstrates Hedda's superior intelligence, her sophistication, and her natural rap-
port with this man of society.

NOTE: In Ibsen's time, such frank and witty talk
was reserved for men. But Hedda would be more
comfortable at the bachelor party Brack is throwing
than George will be. Instead, his wife must sit at
home. It is obvious by now that Hedda's upbringing and taste lean toward masculine society. This
may be a clue why Hedda threatens (literally) men
who approach her as an attractive woman.

Hedda tells Brack that she was bored on her
wedding trip. They speak condescendingly of
George as "a specialist"—a term implying he is
both narrow and dull. But again we see the awk-
wardness of Hedda's position. George bores her
terribly, but he is socially acceptable. She also tells
Brack the true reason for her marriage. Of all her
many admirers, Tesman alone had proposed marriage. None of the others had—perhaps because

she wasn't wealthy, perhaps because they saw she simply wouldn't be a successful wife and mother. Perhaps also they noticed her contemptuous attitude. What do you think? In any case, at twenty-eight she had "danced herself out," and imagined that people were starting to talk. If there's one thing she can't abide, it is looking ridiculous in public. George thus became a "thoroughly acceptable choice."

Here we clearly see a double standard for men and women in society. Neither Hedda nor Brack has a nature that lends itself to intimacy and marriage, but like most women, Hedda feels the weight of social condemnation more than men. She doesn't have the strength it would take to defy convention. Brack, on the other hand, can remain a respectable middle-aged bachelor "with the freedom to come and go" among the compliant wives of his acquaintances. In fact, he wants Hedda to be one of them. Their suggestive conversation about triangular relationships ends indecisively. Is Hedda suggesting she wouldn't mind if she weren't afraid of getting caught? From what you already know of Hedda, is this likely? It's also possible that this kind of "dangerous" flirtation with its lively conversation truly attracts her. It could be said that she leads Brack on, that the game relieves her boredom. Hedda is attracted to people who are "full of life."

When George makes a brief appearance, coming in with a copy of Løvborg's book, Hedda and Brack play verbal games that exclude George entirely. By doing this, they underline Hedda's comradeship with Brack and her alienation from George.

George introduces two distasteful realities that interrupt this verbal game playing between Hedda and Brack: his aunts and Hedda's pregnancy. Hedda again cannot abide anything female, whether it's the domesticity or doting of his elderly aunts or her own pregnancy. When George leaves, she starts pacing the room and then throws herself down in an armchair. She admits to Brack that she purposely insulted Aunt Julie that morning, that "these things come over me. . . . And I can't hold back." Here Ibsen is implying the power of the subconscious and the dark storm that rages inside Hedda. When Brack tells her that she isn't really happy, she agrees. She has no goals, nothing to work for. She went along with marriage out of pity for George, concern for her own future, and lack of conviction. Society and its conventions intimidate her, yet she loathes the falseness. She's uncomfortable and upset at being a female but doesn't dare to express herself as a man would. She contents herself with negative behavior instead of constructive action.

Hedda is an aristocrat who's stuck in this "tight little world" of middle-class society, which makes "life so miserable! So utterly ludicrous!" Brack reminds her that she will soon have a woman's "most solemn responsibility." She replies significantly, "You'll never see me like that!" Is Ibsen giving you a clue about her final action? Hedda snaps, "I won't have responsibilities!" She is responsible for no one and to no one—except her own fear of public scandal. The only thing she has to live for now is the "championship match" between George and Løvborg for the professorship. Instead of a middle-class mother, she will be a courtly medieval lady watching two knights fighting for her favor.

George reenters, dressed for Brack's party. They're still waiting for Løvborg to call in response to George's invitation. Since Løvborg is a reformed alcoholic, Hedda plans to have him spend the evening with her and Thea, instead of going to Brack's bachelor party, where drinks will be served.

Just as they're discussing these plans, Løvborg arrives. Berta announces that he has come to see Hedda. Løvborg's first act goes against convention. It would have been considered odd, if not improper, to ask to see a man's wife if the man were at home, but George doesn't seem to notice.

Finally you get to meet the much-discussed Eilert Løvborg. He is described as pale and thin but wearing a new suit (a cover of respectability?). The first thing you learn about Løvborg is that he is honest; he admits that the book that has restored his reputation is not worthwhile. It was just meant to please the critics.

You also see right away that Løvborg is decent; he will not seek the professorship George is after. He is also sober—in literal fact and in his down-to-earth approach.

Løvborg announces that he is working on a new book that speaks for his "true self," a book on the future of civilization. Unlike Hedda and the others, he has found fulfillment in his "true self." The others have to find their fulfillment outside themselves. For example, George's identity is in his "special field," Thea's is in Løvborg and his writings, and Hedda's, if it exists at all, has yet to be established. A comparison of Løvborg with all the characters up to this point can only point to his superiority.

Løvborg seems determined not to take a drink and declines Brack's invitation to the bachelor party. That is where Hedda makes her move; she invites him to dine with her and Thea Elvsted. There is a sense of foreboding as he accepts. What game does Hedda have in mind? She offers the men a drink. Løvborg refuses. Hedda then gets rid of George and Brack momentarily so that she can talk to Løvborg alone.

Now the central relationship of the play will begin to unfold. It's not surprising that Løvborg touches a deep chord in Hedda. But ask yourself just what it is that touches Hedda. Is it the Løvborg you've just seen or one that Hedda has created?

The two seem at first on the verge of reviving an old relationship. He calls her "Hedda Gabler"— a reminder of the past and her truest identity. They seem close, but when Løvborg attempts to speak of love, she rejects him, pushing him away as she had done before.

What was it about Løvborg that had attracted Hedda in the past? He expresses wonder that she could get him to describe in detail his wild drinking sprees, "the madness that went on day and night. . . ." Is this Hedda's idea of living, the vicarious experience of another's depravity? Or is it only that she wanted to share in the typical male escapades that her boyish upbringing had led her to expect? Løvborg describes their past relationship in terms of companionship and frankness. When he reminds Hedda that he thought her questions about his revels bold, he really means that they were bold *for a woman*.

However, her boldness limited itself to words. In that way the proper Hedda was safe from dreaded scandal. When Løvborg wanted more of a commitment from Hedda, she rejected a man-woman relationship and even threatened to shoot him with one of her father's pistols. She wanted neither intimacy nor scandal. He calls her a coward and she admits it. At the same time she petulantly reminds him that now he has Thea to console him.

When Løvborg makes disparaging remarks about Thea's ability to understand the kind of kinship that existed between him and Hedda, isn't he putting the two of them on a superior level to ordinary people? As you read on, consider in what ways they are different from others and how this affects their lives.

NOTE: Romanticism The nineteenth-century Romantic movement in art and literature cultivated the idea that life was more truly reflected in one's feelings than in "dry" intellectuality. In its more extreme forms, this idea equated creativity and unrestrained emotional expression, even if it meant giving in to destructive impulses. In this view, death was preferable to an unfulfilled, mundane existence. Suicide inspired by failure was a common theme. Both Løvborg and Hedda have Romantic notions that make it difficult for them to get along in the world. To what extent are these notions responsible for their unhappiness? How much are society and individual personality responsible?

But now Hedda wants to reassert her control. Just before Thea arrives, she plays a trump card: She admits that her failure to shoot Løvborg wasn't her "worst cowardice," and implies that she should have had the courage to love him and join him in his quest for life. This ignites his hope once again. After Thea enters, Hedda makes her next move, by identifying the party that Brack and George are going to as "a drinking party." She insists on sitting between Løvborg and Thea, saying honestly, "I want to be in the middle."

Løvborg then raises the stakes by talking about Thea's courage—the attribute Hedda has just admitted she lacks. He insists he and Thea are "true companions. We trust each other completely." This is the basis of their relationship, and this is where Hedda must strike.

First she attacks his private demons. She tries to insist he have a drink, because it's obvious that George and Judge Brack look down on him since he doesn't dare drink. She realizes that public respect is again important to Løvborg, and because of this, he cares a great deal what people think.

Hedda says that people might think Løvborg's not really sure of himself at all. Is he? Some readers feel that Løvborg is himself now because he's found how to harness his brilliance, control himself, and work productively. Others feel he's selling out by coming back to gain favor from the society he holds in contempt. What do you think? Why?

Then Hedda attacks Thea and Løvborg's relationship by hinting that Thea has been frantic because she doesn't trust Løvborg. Thea can't deny it, but she's stricken when she sees how hurt he is. Despite Thea's pleading, Løvborg not only takes a drink, but agrees to go to the judge's party.

NOTE: When Løvborg finds out that Thea was worried because she didn't completely trust him, he says he is glad to know. "Thanks for the truth. Long live truth!" he says as he takes the first fatal drink. The theme that total truth can be destructive recurs in many of Ibsen's plays.

Hedda is thrilled. She wishes she could go with them and be invisible, "to hear a little of your un-adulterated liveliness." She still thinks of "living" in terms of free, uncontrolled behavior. Unwilling to give in to excess herself, she would be satisfied looking on as she had once just listened to Løvborg's stories of his wild life. In Hedda's fantasy, he will return "with vine leaves in his hair—fiery and bold . . . back in control of himself. He'll be a free man, then, for the rest of his days."

NOTE: The image Hedda uses to describe Løvborg's return to unfettered beauty and inner freedom, the "vine leaves in his hair," is a reference to the ancient Greek god of wine and ecstasy. Called Dionysus or Bacchus, the god was associated with poetic and dramatic expression, as well as sexual potency. His followers would engage in wild bouts of drunken revelry and were thought to indulge in human sacrifice accomplished by tearing the victim into pieces. How does this image fit in with Hedda's concept of beauty and freedom?

Although you know that Løvborg's reliance on alcohol is a means of enslavement, not freedom, Hedda's idea of freedom is different. In what sense can freedom from all restraints be considered freedom at all? Hedda considers Løvborg's rehabilitation and return to society a defeat. But if she wants

him to be free, why does she want to substitute
Thea's alleged power over him with her own? Is
Hedda merely being hypocritical, knowing that his
drinking will destroy him? Some readers think she
is primarily motivated by her desire to get even
with Thea whose "power" has been so constructive. Hedda's motivations are not easy to figure
out. By the play's end you may be able to understand this scene better.

ACT THREE

Early the next morning, we find Hedda and Thea
sleeping in the drawing room. They've been there
all night, but neither Løvborg nor George has come
back. When Hedda awakens to learn that no one
has returned she assures Thea that George either
went to his aunts' house or slept at Judge Brack's,
and that Løvborg is "sitting with vine leaves in his
hair, reading away." Thea reluctantly goes off to
bed, and Hedda calls Berta to build up the fire in
the stove. Someone rings the doorbell just as Berta
is putting wood on the fire, so Hedda takes over
while Berta goes to the door.

NOTE: Here you see Hedda literally feeding the
fire. Not only does this illustrate her burning rage
and destructive tendencies, but it foreshadows a
"burning" yet to come.

When George arrives, Hedda tries to find out
what happened at the party. But instead of telling
Hedda what she wants to know, George talks about
Løvborg's remarkable new manuscript.

Then George confesses that he envies Løvborg's
ability. These feelings are so foreign to Tesman
that he is shocked by them. The contrast between
Hedda and her husband is almost funny. She is
such a master of envy and destructive thoughts
that George's feelings seem like child's play. He
then reveals that Løvborg indeed lost control of
himself when the party turned into an orgy. Tesman feels sorry for him, whereas Hedda is still
anticipating a triumph of rebellious creativity. "Were
there vine leaves in his hair?" she asks, knowing
full well that George will be mystified. Løvborg
had apparently given a speech dedicated to the
"woman who'd inspired his work." To whom do
you think Løvborg was referring?

NOTE: Some readers think that Ibsen gives
Løvborg a female inspiration (either Thea or Hedda)
to parallel his own reaction to Emilie Bardach, an
eighteen-year-old girl with whom he carried on a
passionate correspondence. Ibsen called Emilie "the
May sun in a September life." Ibsen abruptly broke
off the correspondence before he wrote this play,
but many readers feel that Hedda's portrait is partly
based on Emilie.

Løvborg had gotten so drunk that he'd dropped
his precious manuscript. George has it and plans
to return it as soon as Løvborg has had a chance
to sleep it off. Tesman knows that such a manuscript is irreplaceable because the "inspiration" often
cannot be recreated. His remark foreshadows the
eventual fate of the manuscript.

George must leave to attend to his dying Aunt

Rina. Hedda refuses to go, claiming she doesn't "want to look on sickness and death. I want to be free of everything ugly." Hedda's attachment to her pistols has already suggested that death holds some attraction for her. Perhaps, in her mind, there are times when death is far from ugly—when it is even beautiful.

Hedda snatches the manuscript from George and hides it just as Judge Brack enters. Alone with Hedda, Brack brings more news of the evening's events. It seems that some of his guests, including Løvborg, left for another party being held at Mademoiselle Diana's, the "redheaded singer" that Thea thought was Løvborg's old flame. Brack calls the woman "a mighty huntress—of men" in a reference to the Roman goddess Diana, who is usually depicted as a huntress.

NOTE: Some readers see Mademoiselle Diana as a third female type, who stands in contrast to both Hedda and Thea. Thea is caring, loving, and supportive, but also attuned to society's demands. Diana, on the other hand, is a "free" woman who rejects society, revels in excess, and accepts her own sexuality. Hedda stands between, possessing the drives of a Diana but restricted by the propriety of a Thea. When Løvborg is in control of his drives, he turns to Thea; when he is not in control, he seeks out Diana. What alternative can Hedda offer?

Brack continues his story. There was a fight at Mademoiselle Diana's when Løvborg claimed he had been robbed there. He was arrested and has now lost all his hard-won respectability. Brack cautions Hedda against seeing him. He senses a rivalry between himself and Løvborg and warns Hedda that he intends to win.

Hedda's dream has been shattered. Instead of "vine leaves" there is only a drunken brawl and public scandal. On top of that, Brack is playing his own power game to make her become his lover. You have already seen that Hedda's pistols don't frighten Brack. He knows her better—and she senses this when she reminds him that he has no hold over her that he could use for blackmail.

When Løvborg finally arrives and forces his way in, over Berta's resistance, he confronts both Hedda and Thea with his sense of total self-defeat. Thea is too late to save him, he admits. There is no more future, no "thirst for life." He won't turn to Thea again. Hedda may be able to salvage something yet.

The whole purpose of Thea's life is threatened without Løvborg and her role as his helpmate. Instead of remaining passive, she becomes angry. She insists on being together with him when the book comes out because it's half hers. Løvborg lies to her and tells her he's torn the manuscript into a thousand pieces and scattered them into the fjord (inlet). "I've torn my own life to bits. So why not tear up my life's work as well—" he comments bitterly. He feels caught in a downward spiral and says that the pieces of paper will sink into the water, "Deeper and deeper. As I will, Thea." Thea is horrified; to her it's like killing their child.

NOTE: The Manuscript "Child" The portrayal of the manuscript as Løvborg's and Thea's child serves several purposes in conveying information about Løvborg, Thea, and Hedda. It reminds you that Thea has given herself to Løvborg physically and mentally in a way that Hedda is unable; also, that Thea, who has no real children of her own, has created a beloved "child," while Hedda hates the thought of the real child she is producing as well as the intellectual products of George's mind. Despite Thea's apparent physical barrenness, she is a fertile, pro-life force, while Hedda, with all her physical fertility is a barren vessel.

Thea can only respond to Løvborg's act of "murder" by leaving him and predicting "darkness ahead." Considering his behavior, how do you react to his accusation against Thea, that she has "broken" his "courage and daring for life"? Doesn't this sound like Hedda's view of things? How can he equate his violent return to alcohol with courage or daring? Is he feeling sorry for himself, realizing what a mess he's made of things? Is he trying once again to enlist Hedda as a supporter? It is interesting to note that, despite some of their differences, George and Løvborg share not only an intellectual orientation, but a dependency on women. Is Ibsen trying to say something about men in general? How does Brack's desire for Hedda figure in, if at all?

Hedda is still resentful of Thea's power. She has no intention of telling Løvborg that she has his "lost" manuscript—especially when he tells her that "Thea's pure soul was in that book." By hiding the manuscript, Hedda can keep him from Thea. And by getting him to fulfill her notion of beauty and freedom, she can then keep him forever. Instead of "vine leaves" (her symbol of a free, poetic spirit), she now seeks a "beautiful" end for him. Can any death be beautiful?

You have already seen Hedda's morbid fascination with destruction. Her pistols seem her only means of self-expression. Whether they represent her incessant boredom (her only talent—"boring myself to death," she once remarked) or her destructive impulses or perhaps even her masculine nature (in which men, guns, and power are equivalent), the inevitable conclusion seems to be death. Since Hedda also believes that freedom and creativity mean throwing off the restraints of a dull society, what better way to take ultimate control than by making a decision to reject life altogether? If you can't create on your own, you can at least die by your own hand.

The pistols and Hedda's version of freedom converge as she goes to the writing table and gets one of her father's guns, the "souvenir" she has just promised Løvborg. Instead of giving him the manuscript—his "child" that signifies life and the future—she hands him death—a pistol. He takes the gun and leaves.

Hedda goes back to the writing desk and gets out the manuscript. Without a sign of remorse, she starts to throw the pages on the fire. Her jealousy and destructiveness are shown clearly as she addresses her rival: "Now I'm burning your child, Thea! You, with your curly hair! Your child and Eilert Løvborg's. Now I'm burning—I'm burning the child."

In quick succession, Hedda has indulged in two destructive acts. Her negative impulses have taken over, and she appears powerful and triumphant.

The fourth and final act will strip Hedda of her last illusions.

ACT FOUR

The final act begins in darkness. Although it's evening, no lamps are lit. Hedda is alone. Dressed in mourning, she prowls and paces restlessly, then moves into the inner room and plays some chords on her piano.

NOTE: You'll remember that Hedda's old piano is a reminder of her early freedom and status as General Gabler's daughter. It is also a reminder of death. Ibsen often links music and death, especially in the context of the Dionysian orgies (bacchanalia) of ancient mythology. (See the Note on page 96.) In *A Doll's House*, a frenzied piano accompaniment to a dance is a prelude to Dr. Rank's death and Nora's death plans. In Act Three, Løvborg's orgy at Mademoiselle Diana's preceded his desire for death. Now Hedda goes to the piano in mourning clothes. Whose death has occurred; whose death will follow?

Aunt Julie appears, also in mourning, to report what you may have already deduced: Aunt Rina has died. But Hedda is no doubt awaiting news of Løvborg's suicide.

NOTE: The blackness and the mourning at the beginning of this act emphasize that all the char-

acters except Hedda and Judge Brack have already
lost the things that gave meaning to their life.
Løvborg has lost both his manuscript and his self-
respect; Thea has lost Løvborg and her "child" (the
manuscript); George has lost respect for his obviously inferior work; and Aunt Juliana has lost
Rina (to death) and George (to marriage). Even the
servant Berta has lost her old home with the mis-
tresses she loved. Only Hedda and Brack still have
plans for something better at this point.

George comes in uncharacteristically preoccupied. For some reason, this man who's spent his
life caring about his aunts has practically forgotten
that one of them has died! Hedda, just as surprisingly, is the one consoling Aunt Julie and noting
that it will be lonely for her. Aunt Julie, as you
would expect, fusses over the details of Rina's fu-
neral. Although she's upset, Aunt Julie is practical
and seems to realize that life goes on. She announces her intention to take in a boarder, "some
poor invalid in need of care and attention."

When Aunt Julie leaves, George confesses the
true reason for his concern. He couldn't find
Løvborg to tell him about the manuscript and has
found out from Thea that Hedda didn't tell Løvborg
where it was. Now George is afraid Løvborg will
harm himself. He wants to take the book to him
immediately.

Hedda coolly tells George she doesn't have it
any more; she's burned it. George is stunned. He
reacts just like a "specialist": "It's illegal disposi-
tion of lost property!" But then he demands to
know why she did such a thing. Hedda, who is
practiced in the art of being devious, says she did

it for him, because he had admitted he was envious and she didn't want anyone to stand in his way.

George is so innocent that he's almost convinced by Hedda's reasoning. Hedda then makes the most of her wifely role by confirming that she's pregnant. But just admitting her condition sends Hedda into despair. She clenches her fists and cries, "Oh, I'll die—I'll die of all this!"

George doesn't really know what she means but is overwhelmed by these first signs of "love" from Hedda. Suddenly, she is carrying his child, calling him by his first name, and burning manuscripts for him! "I wonder, really, if things such as this are common among young wives? Hm?" Hedda sarcastically tells him he'd better ask Aunt Julie.

Thea and Judge Brack arrive almost simultaneously with news about Løvborg. He has been taken to the hospital and is dying. It seems he shot himself in the chest (not in the temple, the traditional heroic mode of suicide that Hedda had envisioned when she handed him the pistol). She's triumphant nonetheless: "At last, something truly done! . . . there's beauty in all this!"

If the play ended here, Hedda would have won. She would have finally exercised power over someone. But no sooner has Hedda claimed one victory than another is snatched away from her.

George and Thea decide to recreate Løvborg's destroyed book from his notes, which she had kept. Knowing that Hedda burned the manuscript, George feels he owes this act to the dying man. They go off immediately to begin work.

Some readers feel this turn of events strains credibility. How is it that Thea has the notes with her? She certainly doesn't seem as upset as she should be about Løvborg, for whom she chucked respectability. How can she be so excited about a manuscript when he is dying? Some might say that she never cared for Løvborg as a person. Like Aunt Juliana, anyone needing aid will do, or any noble work is equal to another. How do you react to Thea's new project?

When Thea and George have left the room, Brack shatters Hedda's last illusion. For Thea's sake, he hadn't told exactly what had happened. The truth is, Løvborg didn't commit suicide; it was an accident. He didn't shoot himself in the chest but in the stomach. And the shooting had happened at Mademoiselle Diana's.

Hedda is in despair. Far from an act of courage and freedom, it was a stupid mishap in a sordid setting. Far from being a "beautiful" shot in the temple, it was an ugly shot in the stomach. Hedda, defeated, asks, "What is it, this—this curse—that everything I touch turns ridiculous and vile?" Do you have an answer?

Hedda now faces what she can least stand— scandal. Brack recognized Hedda's pistol and proposes a little blackmail. If this became known, she would be involved in a messy, public case. If she doesn't want Brack to talk, she must agree to become his mistress.

NOTE: Some readers feel that Hedda's vulnerability to Brack's blackmail is not believable. After all, Hedda has never hesitated to lie before. Even if she doesn't want to say that Løvborg stole the gun, she could claim she'd given it to him for some innocent purpose. Others, however, feel that Hedda's extreme sensitivity to scandal has been clear from the beginning and that even having her name linked to the case would be unacceptable to her.

Now Hedda's loss of power is an inescapable fact. She is caught in a double bind. To keep herself from one scandalous situation, she must participate in another. Brack has her in his power. Even her distorted fantasies of freedom are impossible now.

To underscore the futility of her existence, George and Thea return and take her place at the writing table, because there isn't enough "light" in the inner room. Remember that the inner room symbolizes Hedda's true self. For a final question, Hedda asks George, "Is there nothing the two of you need from me now?" Her husband seals her fate by answering, "No, nothing in the world." Hedda has become totally superfluous.

Hedda goes into the inner room and plays a frenzied dance on the piano. Here is the ritual, the "bacchanalia" before death. George doesn't understand the connection and asks Hedda to stop. "Think of Auntie Rina! And Eilert, too!" Hedda assures him that she *is* thinking of them. She promises, "From now on I'll be quiet." A short time later a pistol shot rings out. The others rush in to find Hedda shot in the temple. Judge Brack closes the play, ironically, with his remark, "But good God! People don't *do* such things!"—a paraphrase of Hedda's comment to Thea in Act One: "Nobody behaves that way around here." Hedda's death has been her one (and only) courageous act against society.

NOTE: Hedda's Death   Hedda's suicide is one of the most controversial play endings in theatrical history. What does it mean?

To some, Hedda's death is a triumph. At last she has had the strength to do "one free and courageous action" that "shimmers with spontaneous beauty." Instead of trying to manipulate others to act, Hedda has herself finally acted. She has broken free of the stodgy, conventional middle-class society she despised. Her final act typifies a true aristocratic nature because it cares more about the gesture than the consequences.

Others see Hedda's death as the ultimate tragedy in a sterile and disturbed life. She has finally done something that she considers beautiful, but it is totally negative. She has never known satisfaction, never fulfilled her own nature, never acted constructively. Instead she has spent her whole life torn between fear and anger, seeking triumph, but gaining only despair. She has wasted her energy on supposed victories over others.

It has also been pointed out that the most notable thing about Hedda's suicide is that it arouses neither pity nor anger in the readers or playgoers. By the end, some care little about this frustrated, neurotic woman, despite her problems. Could it be because she never even tries to fight against her worse nature? Hedda is not a passionate fighter for herself or even against her supposed enemies. To many she is a case study of a father-dominated, deeply disturbed personality whose death is less moving than inevitable. She is incapable of evoking sympathy.

How you react to this portrait of Hedda will inevitably color your view of this play. Are her motivations clear? In commenting on Hedda, Ibsen suggested that she was an example of a person who failed to realize her potential. Is this how you see her? Also, consider the question whether a character who doesn't change is really interesting.

These are only a few of the questions this play inspires. You will have your own, no doubt. Perhaps the very fact that you are left with such questions is an indication of the interest *Hedda Gabler* continues to generate.

A STEP BEYOND

Test and Answers

TEST

1. Convention and the society Hedda hates _____
   are embodied by
   A. Løvborg and Thea
   B. Aunt Juliana and George   C. Brack

2. Hedda insults Aunt Juliana's hat because _____
   A. she hates it when Aunt Juliana puts
      on airs
   B. hats symbolize femininity
   C. she can't help it

3. "Vine leaves" are symbolic of _____
   A. pagan freedom, poetry, and defiance
   B. Løvborg's classical education
   C. a death crown

4. Brack holds back the following information _____
   about Løvborg's shooting
   I. where it occurred
   II. the seriousness of his condition
   III. where the bullet struck him
   A. I and III only   B. I and II only
   C. I, II, and III

5. Løvborg is most interested in _____
   A. a moral victory
   B. the professorship
   C. the success of his book

6. George's slippers signify _____

   A. how much at home he feels with
      Hedda
   B. his attachment to his aunts
   C. that he's a creature of habit

7. Hedda says her greatest talent is for   _____
   A. making others miserable
   B. riding and shooting
   C. boring herself to death

8. Thea's attitude toward Hedda is mostly   _____
one of
   A. awe   B. gratitude   C. fear

9. Thea shows her courage and defiance by   _____
   A. slapping Hedda
   B. leaving her husband
   C. rewriting Løvborg's manuscript

10. Hedda shoots herself   _____
   I. to defy society
  II. as an act of beauty
 III. because she has no reason to live
   A. I, II, and III   B. III only
   C. I and II only

11. Discuss the significance of the play's title.

12. Discuss the gap between Hedda's convictions and
her actions.

13. Explain the significance of having a "child" for Hedda
and for Thea.

14. Discuss Ibsen's attitude toward selflessness. Give
examples.

15. Is Hedda's death a triumph or a defeat? Defend your
answer.

ANSWERS

1. B **2.** C **3.** A **4.** C **5.** A **6.** B
7. C **8.** C **9.** B **10.** A

11. You might explain that Hedda's sense of identity is based on her past rather than on her present. Her marriage to George Tesman means nothing to her except a position in society. She is still shaped by and obedient to her deceased father, General Gabler, who instilled in her a man's consciousness in a woman's body. Symbols of her father's dominance include his portrait and his pistols. He determined Hedda's attitude toward rank and power and caused her hatred of weakness or femininity. His class, the aristocracy, also gave Hedda her ideas about noble gestures and honor, and probably her distaste for the middle class. Putting a bullet in one's temple is an acceptable death in matters of honor.

12. Hedda yearns to be free, yet she is unable to pay the price for that freedom. To be truly free she must know herself, but she has been cut off from all that is feminine or creative within herself—and has even been taught to despise it. She must instead settle for having power over others who do have courage and creativity.

Moreover, she hates society and longs to defy it. But she is paralyzed by her fear of scandal and the dread of looking ridiculous. She wants to join Løvborg in his wild sprees, assert her "poetry," think daring thoughts, and be aggressive. But all she allows herself is to threaten people with her father's pistols.

Hedda can see that it would take courage to commit herself to intimacy with someone like Løvborg, and she refuses to do it. She knows she will never find happiness as a coward, but she does not have the resources or courage to free herself or to act.

13. Note that a child represents different things to different characters in the play. To Aunt Julie, a child symbolizes another dependent human being to take care of; to Thea, it symbolizes the product of a collaboration of love; to Brack, it symbolizes responsibility; to George, it symbolizes (mistakenly) his wife's love for him.

To Hedda, a child signifies femininity, responsibility, and the continuation of life. There is nothing she detests more. If she carries her baby to term, she will have admitted her femaleness, the reality of her marriage to George, and her responsibility for another human being. Against her will—indeed, against her very nature—she will have been part of a positive, creative, and constructive force. She has to destroy the child, even if it means destroying herself.

By the same token, the manuscript "child" of Thea and Løvborg symbolizes the union between them, a union Hedda wants to usurp and destroy. For dramatic purposes, Ibsen has Hedda destroy the manuscript to remove any chance that Løvborg could recover it and possibly redeem himself. Also, destroying it throws Thea and Tesman together and puts Hedda at Brack's mercy.

14. The play's attitudes toward selflessness are best illustrated by Aunt Juliana and Thea Elvsted. Aunt Juliana is so selfless that she brings up orphaned George, cares for her invalid sister, and plans to take in another helpless person. It can be argued that this is really a way to keep others dependent on her, keep herself busy, and make sure she never has to know or deal with her true self. By the same token, it can be argued that Thea helps Løvborg not out of love but out of selfishness. It gives her a sense of self, a sense of power, and a sense of accomplishment. She is easily able to get those same rewards with George not even an hour after Løvborg dies.

Even though the helping hands of Thea and Aunt

Juliana have created dependency, there seem to be few alternatives. Løvborg can't manage on his own without getting drunk, and he isn't very productive when he drinks. Hedda can't act on her own either, nor can George. Maybe a certain amount of selflessness is necessary.

15. If you feel Hedda's death is a triumph, you can point out that through the whole play she has equated violence with beauty. With her suicide, she has achieved a spontaneous act of beauty. Also, instead of manipulating others to act, Hedda has finally acted herself. She has defied society and outwitted Brack.

If you feel Hedda's death is a defeat, you can point out the obvious: all death is defeat. Also, no one appreciates the beauty of her action. She has never known herself, never accepted love, never done anything constructive. This act quenches her thirst for life. She has spent her life hurting others and denying their validity. Her own end is a relief to all concerned.

Another way to look at this is to consider whether Hedda's death isn't inevitable. Isn't it foreshadowed in the first description of Hedda ("pallid and opaque"—like the face of a corpse?) and in the description of the drawing room ("decorated in dark colors") and the trees ("in autumn colors")? If you consider her death inevitable, how does this affect the idea of "triumph" or "defeat"?

Term Paper Ideas and other Topics for Writing

Hedda

1. Hedda Gabler: a psychological portrait.
2. Hedda Gabler as a reflection of Henrik Ibsen.

3. A comparison of Hedda Gabler and Gustave Flaubert's Emma Bovary.

4. Hedda Gabler: the product of a masculine society.

Themes

1. Orgies and death in *A Doll's House* and *Hedda Gabler*.

2. The meaning of children in *Hedda Gabler*.

3. Self-realization in *Hedda Gabler*.

4. Society versus the individual in *Hedda Gabler*.

5. Hedda and her father.

6. Romanticism in *Hedda Gabler*.

The Play

1. Visual symbolism in *Hedda Gabler*.

2. *Hedda Gabler:* tragedy or case history?

3. Interpretations of Hedda's death.

Other Characters

1. Tesman and Løvborg: a comparison of two scholars.

2. Løvborg's three women.

3. Ibsen's techniques of revealing character in *Hedda Gabler* and *A Doll's House*.

A Doll's House
and
Hedda Gabler

Further Reading
CRITICAL WORKS

Beyer, Edward. *Ibsen: The Man and His Work*. New York: Taplinger, 1980. Complete, easy-to-read overview of Ibsen's life and plays.

Bradbrook, M. C. *Ibsen the Norwegian*. Hamden, Conn.: Archon Books, 1969 (first published 1948). Practical discussion of the plays and their context.

Brandès, Georg. *Henrik Ibsen*. New York: B. Blom, 1964 (first published 1899). Interesting commentary by one of Ibsen's contemporaries.

Downs, Brian W. *A Study of Six Plays by Ibsen*. Cambridge, Eng.: Cambridge University Press, 1950. Includes an interesting study of *A Doll's House*.

Durback, Errol. *Ibsen the Romantic*. Athens, Ga.: Univ. of Georgia Press, 1982. A scholarly treatise on Ibsen's later works.

Gray, Ronald. *Ibsen—A Dissenting View*. Cambridge, Eng.: Cambridge University Press, 1980. Raises some commonsense questions about Ibsen's plays.

Ibsen, Henrik. *Letters and Speeches*. Edited by Evert Sprinchorn. New York: Hill and Wang, 1964. Searing comments and insights from Ibsen himself.

Jorgenson, Theodore. *Henrik Ibsen: His Life and Drama*. Ann Arbor, Mich.: Edwards Brothers, 1963. Good interpretive discussion of the plays.

Lucas, F. L. *The Drama of Ibsen and Strindberg*. New York: Macmillan, 1962. Practical and readable discussions of each play.

Meyer, Hans Georg. *Henrik Ibsen*. New York: Frederick Ungar, 1972. Examines the moral issues in the plays.

Shaw, George Bernard. *The Quintessence of Ibsenism*. New York: Hill and Wang, 1957 (first published 1913). A classic work by the great dramatist who helped bring Ibsen international acclaim.

AUTHOR'S OTHER MAJOR WORKS

Love's Comedy (1862)
Brand (1866)
Peer Gynt (1867)
Emperor and Galilean (1873)
The Pillars of Society (1877)
Ghosts (1881)
An Enemy of the People (1882)
The Wild Duck (1884)
Rosmersholm (1886)
The Lady from the Sea (1888)
The Master Builder (1892)
Little Eyolf (1894)
John Gabriel Borkman (1896)
When We Dead Awaken (1899)

The Critics

Ibsen's Contribution

Shakespear had put ourselves on the stage but not our situations. . . . Ibsen supplies the want left by Shakespear. He gives us not only ourselves but our situations. The things that happen to his stage figures are things that happen to us. One consequence is that his plays are much more important to us than

Shakespear's. Another is that they are capable both of hurting us cruelly and of filling us with excited hopes of escape from idealistic tyrannies and with visions of intenser life in the future.

—*George Bernard Shaw*, The
Quintessence of Ibsenism, *1913*

A Doll's House—Its Place in History

A Doll's House almost irresistibly invites sweeping generalizations. It is the first Modern Tragedy, as Ibsen originally named it. The strong divorce play and the social drama are alike descended from it. *A Doll's House* stands in relation to modern drama as Queen Victoria to the royal families of Europe. It is not Ibsen's greatest play, but it is probably his most striking achievement, in the sense that it changed most decisively the course of literature. Its significance for contemporaries is quite distinct from its permanent significance or, again, from its place in the personal development of Ibsen as an artist.

—*M. C. Bradbrook*, Ibsen the
Norwegian, *1948*

Nora as a Tragic Heroine

'The modern tragedy' does not end in ruin, as Ibsen originally had intended, but in a new start. However, values are destroyed as the whole of Nora's world collapses. This happens precisely because she is true to the best in herself. She grows in stature, and is purged by suffering. In defeat she is victorious. In the majority of theories about 'the tragic' these are significant factors. When everything lies in ruins round her, Nora emerges strong and independent as never before, and takes the consequences of her newly gained understanding; she is in the process of becoming 'herself'; at the same time she points to a freer and more honest humanity in a healthier society. It is in this sense that she is a modern, tragic heroine, and the play precisely what it claims to be, a 'modern tragedy'.

—*Edward Beyer*, Ibsen: The Man
and His Work, *1980*